Third Workshop on Simple and Efficient Natural Language Processing (SustaiNLP 2022)

Abu Dhabi, United Arab Emirates
7 December 2022

ISBN: 978-1-7138-9149-9

Printed from e-media with permission by:

Curran Associates, Inc.
57 Morehouse Lane
Red Hook, NY 12571

Some format issues inherent in the e-media version may also appear in this print version.

Printed with permission by Curran Associates, Inc. (2024)

For permission requests, please contact the Association for Computational Linguistics
at the address below.

Association for Computational Linguistics
209 N. Eighth Street
Stroudsburg, Pennsylvania 18360

Phone: 1-570-476-8006
Fax: 1-570-476-0860

acl@aclweb.org

Additional copies of this publication are available from:

Curran Associates, Inc.
57 Morehouse Lane
Red Hook, NY 12571 USA
Phone: 845-758-0400
Fax: 845-758-2633
Email: curran@proceedings.com
Web: www.proceedings.com

SustaiNLP 2022

The Third Workshop on Simple and Efficient Natural Language Processing

Proceedings of the Workshop

December 7, 2022

Introduction

It is our great pleasure to welcome you to the third edition of SustaiNLP: Workshop on Simple and Efficient Natural Language Processing.

The Natural Language Processing community has, in recent years, demonstrated a notable focus on improving higher scores on standard benchmarks and taking the lead on community-wide leaderboards (e.g., GLUE, SentEval). While this aspiration has led to improvements in benchmark performance of (predominantly neural) models, it has also came at a cost, i.e., increased model complexity and the ever-growing amount of computational resources required for training and using the current state-of-the-art models. Moreover, the recent research efforts have, for the most part, failed to identify sources of empirical gains in models, often failing to empirically justify the model complexity beyond benchmark performance.

Because of these easily observable trends, we organized the SustaiNLP workshop with the goal of promoting more sustainable NLP research and practices, with two main objectives: (1) encouraging development of more efficient NLP models; and (2) providing simpler architectures and empirical justification of model complexity. For both aspects, we encouraged submissions from all topical areas of NLP.

Besides the original research papers (short and long), we encouraged cross-submissions of work that has been published at other events as well as extended abstracts of work in progress that fit the scope and aims of the workshop (only the original research papers, however, are included in these workshop proceedings).

This year, we received 17 submissions from ARR, proposing a multitude of viable resource-efficient NLP methods and spanning a wide range of NLP applications. We have selected 8 submissions for presentation at the workshop, yielding an acceptance rate of 47%.

Many thanks to the ARR program committee and our senior area chairs for their thorough and thoughtful reviews. We would also like to thank to our panelists and invited speakers whose discussions and talks we strongly believe will make the workshop exciting and memorable.

We are looking forward to the third edition of the SustaiNLP workshop!

SustaiNLP Organizers
November 2022

Organizing Committee

Organizers

Angela Fan, INRIA Nancy and Facebook AI Research
Iryna Gurevych, TU Darmstadt
Yufang Hou, IBM Research Ireland
Zornitsa Kozareva, Facebook AI Research
Sasha Luccioni, HuggingFace Inc.
Nafise Sadat Moosavi, University of Sheffield
Sujith Ravi, SliceX AI
Gyuwan Kim, UC Santa Barbara
Roy Schwartz, Hebrew University of Jerusalem
Andreas Rücklé, Amazon Search Berlin

Program Committee

Senior Area Chairs

Daniil Sorokin, Amazon Development Center Germany
Leon Derczynski, IT University
Diego Marcheggiani, Amazon
Nishant Subramani, Allen Institute for Artificial Intelligence
Gabriel Stanovsky, Hebrew University of Jerusalem
Emma Strubell, Carnegie Mellon University and Google

Invited Speakers

Kurt Keutzer, UC Berkeley
Percy Liang, Stanford University
Hinrich Schütze, University of Munich
Song Han, MIT EECS

Panelists

Kurt Keutzer, UC Berkeley
Percy Liang, Stanford University
Hinrich Schütze, University of Munich
Sam Bowman, New York University
Barbara Plank, University of Munich
Scott Wen-tau Yih, Meta AI - FAIR

Table of Contents

Program

Wednesday, December 7, 2022

09:00 - 10:30 *Opening Remarks and Gather Town Session 1*

Improving the Sample Efficiency of Prompt Tuning with Domain Adaptation
Xu Guo, Boyang Li and Han Yu

Partitioned Gradient Matching-based Data Subset Selection for Compute-Efficient Robust ASR Training
Ashish Mittal, Durga Sivasubramanian, Rishabh Iyer, Preethi Jyothi and Ganesh Ramakrishnan

Thinking about GPT-3 In-Context Learning for Biomedical IE? Think Again
Bernal Jimenez Gutierrez, Nikolas McNeal, Clayton Washington, You Chen, Lang Li, Huan Sun and Yu Su

Summarization as Indirect Supervision for Relation Extraction
Keming Lu, I-Hung Hsu, Wenxuan Zhou, Mingyu Derek Ma and Muhao Chen

Bridging the Training-Inference Gap for Dense Phrase Retrieval
Gyuwan Kim, Jinhyuk Lee, Barlas Oguz, Wenhan Xiong, Yizhe Zhang, Yashar Mehdad and William Yang Wang

Ensemble Transformer for Efficient and Accurate Ranking Tasks: an Application to Question Answering Systems
Yoshitomo Matsubara, Luca Soldaini, Eric Lind and Alessandro Moschitti

Plug-and-Play VQA: Zero-shot VQA by Conjoining Large Pretrained Models with Zero Training
Anthony Meng Huat Tiong, Junnan Li, Boyang Li, Silvio Savarese and Steven C.H. Hoi

Train Flat, Then Compress: Sharpness-Aware Minimization Learns More Compressible Models
Clara Na, Sanket Vaibhav Mehta and Emma Strubell

Sparse Mixers: Combining MoE and Mixing to build a more efficient BERT
James Lee-Thorp and Joshua Ainslie

XDoc: Unified Pre-training for Cross-Format Document Understanding
Jingye Chen, Tengchao Lv, Lei Cui, Cha Zhang and Furu Wei

Scaling Laws Under the Microscope: Predicting Transformer Performance from Small Scale Experiments
Maor Ivgi, Yair Carmon and Jonathan Berant

Wednesday, December 7, 2022 (continued)

11:00 - 12:00 *Oral Presentation 1*

Quadapter: Adapter for GPT-2 Quantization
Minseop Park, Jaeseong You, Markus Nagel and Simyung Chang

AfroLM: A Self-Active Learning-based Multilingual Pretrained Language Model for 23 African Languages
Bonaventure F. P. Dossou, Atnafu Lambebo Tonja, Oreen Yousuf, Salomey Osei, Abigail Oppong, Iyanuoluwa Shode, Oluwabusayo Olufunke Awoyomi and Chris Chinenye Emezue

Who Says Elephants Can't Run: Bringing Large Scale MoE Models into Cloud Scale Production
Young Jin Kim, Rawn Henry, Raffy Fahim and Hany Hassan

Effective Pretraining Objectives for Transformer-based Autoencoders
Luca Di Liello, Matteo Gabburo and Alessandro Moschitti

14:30 - 15:00 *Invited Talk (Hinrich Schutze)*

15:00 - 15:30 *Oral Presentation 2*

Algorithmic Diversity and Tiny Models: Comparing Binary Networks and the Fruit Fly Algorithm on Document Representation Tasks
Tanise Ceron, Nhut Truong and Aurelie Herbelot

Scaling Laws Under the Microscope: Predicting Transformer Performance from Small Scale Experiments
Maor Ivgi, Yair Carmon and Jonathan Berant

16:00 - 17:30 *Gather Town Session 2*

Efficient Two-Stage Progressive Quantization of BERT
Charles Le, Arash Ardakani, Amir Ardakani, Hang Zhang, Yuyan Chen, James J. Clark, Brett H. Meyer and Warren J. Gross

KGRefiner: Knowledge Graph Refinement for Improving Accuracy of Translational Link Prediction Methods
Mohammad Javad Saeedizade, Najmeh Torabian and Behrouz Minaei-Bidgoli

Algorithmic Diversity and Tiny Models: Comparing Binary Networks and the Fruit Fly Algorithm on Document Representation Tasks
Tanise Ceron, Nhut Truong and Aurelie Herbelot

HyperMixer: An MLP-based Green AI Alternative to Transformers
Florian Mai, Arnaud Pannatier, Fabio James Fehr, Haolin Chen, Francois Marelli, François Fleuret and James Henderson

A Few More Examples May Be Worth Billions of Parameters
Yuval Kirstain, Patrick Lewis, Sebastian Riedel and Omer Levy

Few-shot initializing of Active Learner via Meta-Learning
Zi Long Zhu, Vikrant Yadav, Zubair Afzal and George Tsatsaronis

From Mimicking to Integrating: Knowledge Integration for Pre-Trained Language Models
Lei Li, Yankai Lin, Xuancheng Ren, Guangxiang Zhao, Peng Li, Jie Zhou and Xu Sun

FPT: Improving Prompt Tuning Efficiency via Progressive Training
Yufei Huang, Yujia Qin, Huadong Wang, Yichun Yin, Maosong Sun, Zhiyuan Liu and Qun Liu

Modeling Context With Linear Attention for Scalable Document-Level Translation
Zhaofeng Wu, Hao Peng, Nikolaos Pappas and Noah A. Smith

Quadapter: Adapter for GPT-2 Quantization
Minseop Park, Jaeseong You, Markus Nagel and Simyung Chang

Towards Realistic Low-resource Relation Extraction: A Benchmark with Empirical Baseline Study
Xin Xu, Xiang Chen, Ningyu Zhang, Xin Xie, Xi Chen and Huajun Chen

DORE: Document Ordered Relation Extraction based on Generative Framework
Qipeng Guo, Yuqing Yang, Hang Yan, Xipeng Qiu and Zheng Zhang

On the Curious Case of l2 norm of Sense Embeddings
Yi Zhou and Danushka Bollegala

Generating Multiple-Length Summaries via Reinforcement Learning for Unsupervised Sentence Summarization
Dongmin Hyun, Xiting Wang, Chayoung Park, Xing Xie and Hwanjo Yu

Explore Unsupervised Structures in Pretrained Models for Relation Extraction
Xi Yang, Tao Ji and Yuanbin Wu

Improving Generalization of Pre-trained Language Models via Stochastic Weight Averaging
Phillippe Langlais, Ali Ghodsi, Ahmad Rashid, Mehdi Rezagholizadeh, Ivan Kobyzev and Peng Lu

Continuation KD: Improved Knowledge Distillation through the Lens of Continuation Optimization
Ali Ghodsi, Pascal Poupart, Mehdi Rezagholizadeh, Ivan Kobyzev and Aref Jafari

Effective Pretraining Objectives for Transformer-based Autoencoders
Luca Di Liello, Matteo Gabburo and Alessandro Moschitti

19:00 - 20:00 *Invited Talk (Song Han)*

20:00 - 20:30 *Panel Discussion*

21:00 - 21:30 *Invited Talk (Percy Liang)*

21:30 - 22:00 *Invited Talk (Kurt Keutzer)*

22:00 - 22:30 *Best Paper Awards and Closing Remarks*

Efficient Two-Stage Progressive Quantization of BERT

Phuoc-Hoan Charles Le, Arash Ardakani, Amir Ardakani, Hang Zhang, Yuyan Chen, James J. Clark, Brett H. Meyer, Warren J. Gross
McGill University
Montreal, Canada

Abstract

The success of large BERT models has raised the demand for model compression methods to reduce model size and computational cost. Quantization can reduce the model size and inference latency, making inference more efficient, without changing its stucture, but it comes at the cost of performance degradation. Due to the complex loss landscape of ternarized/binarized BERT, we present an efficient two-stage progressive quantization method in which we fine tune the model with quantized weights and progressively lower its bitwidth, and then we fine tune the model with quantized weights and activations. At the same time, we strategically choose which bitwidth to fine-tune on and to initialize from, and which bitwidth to fine-tune under augmented data to outperform the existing BERT binarization methods without adding an extra module, compressing the binary model 18% more than previous binarization methods or compressing BERT by 31x w.r.t. to the full-precision model. Without data augmentation, we can outperform existing BERT ternarization methods.

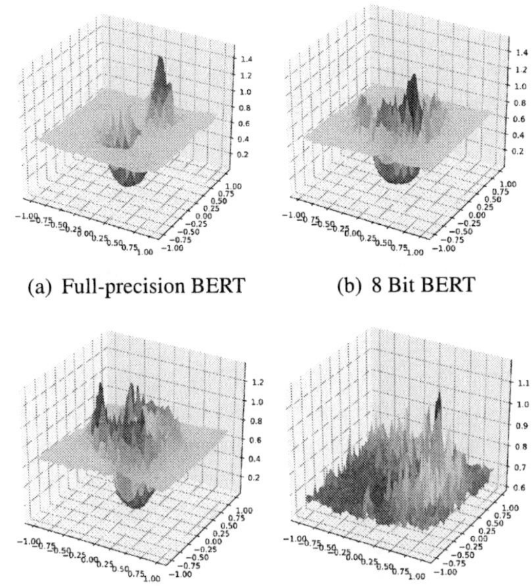

(a) Full-precision BERT (b) 8 Bit BERT
(c) 4 Bit BERT (d) Ternary BERT

Figure 1: Loss landscape of the BERT model on the MRPC dataset with different weight bits.

1 Introduction

BERT (Devlin et al., 2019) models have demonstrated remarkable performance on NLP tasks. However, their memory and high computational cost make it difficult to fit them onto edge devices with limited resources for inference.

Recently, a number of methods have been developed to reduce the number of trainable parameters of BERT such as (Sun et al., 2020; Jiao et al., 2020). However, some edge devices require low-precision models for deployment due to the structure of their arithmetic units (Cortex-M, 2020). Therefore, quantization of BERT-based models is needed to avoid/minimize costly floating-point operations.

Previous works have tried to quantize BERT models. TernaryBERT (Zhang et al., 2020) used knowledge distillation to transfer the knowledge of the full-precision BERT to a BERT model with weights that are ternarized into $\{-1, 0, 1\}$ using 2 bits. BinaryBERT (Bai et al., 2021) binarized the weights into $\{-1, 1\}$ using 1 bit by exploiting the adaptive width property of DynaBERT (Hou et al., 2020) using a method called ternary weight splitting. BiBERT (Qin et al., 2022) managed to outperform (Bai et al., 2021) when binarizing acitvations and binarizing weights. However, there is always a performance loss associated with all the aforementioned methods when using ternary weights and to keep competitive performance, data augmentation from (Jiao et al., 2020) is needed, requiring up to 60x more data as shown in Table 8. For binary weights, the architecture is also modified and an extra module is added and with BiBERT's method alone it cannot reach the full precision performance.

Proceedings of The Third Workshop on Simple and Efficient Natural Language Processing (SustaiNLP), pages 1 - 9
December 7, 2022

More details will be explained on Appendix E on the BiBERT on non binary activations and weights.

A binarized/ternarized BERT has a lot more complex landscape than a full-precision BERT (Bai et al., 2021) as shown in Figure 1, so training ternary/binary model from scratch could cause the model to get trapped in a poor local minima. Therefore, we use a two-stage progressive quantization method inspired by (Zhuang et al., 2018). In the first stage, we progressively lower the bitwidth of weights, and subsequently fine-tune the model. More specifically, the model with a larger bitwidth is used to initialize the model for fine-tuning on a smaller bitwidth of weights. After reaching the best performance with quantized weights (e.g., binary weights), the BERT model is then fine-tuned with quantized activations as the second stage of the quantization method. Activations are also progressively quantized until the desired quantization bitwidth in a similar fashion.

However, for example, applying the method from (Zhuang et al., 2018) to ternarize BERT, naively, costs too much time (or up to 1.67x longer than necessary) with data augmentation used for every bitwidth of weights, with no performance gain as shown in Table 3. We therefore propose an efficient two-stage progressive quantization (ETSPQ) method in which we choose which bitwidth to progressively fine-tune on and which bitwidth to fine-tune under augmented data to save training time and achieve the best possible performance.

We are the first to ternarize the weights of BERT, compressing it by 14.9x while outperforming the full-precision model performance across nearly all GLUE datasets and without data augmentation it can outperform existing BERT ternarization methods. Also, we outperform the state-of-the-art BERT binarization in performance without adding an extra module, compressing the model 18% more than (Bai et al., 2021).

2 Preliminaries

A quantized model has a set of full precision weights, $\mathbf{w}$. For the forward pass, a quantization function from (Li et al., 2016) is used to ternarize each element w_i in the weight matrix $\mathbf{w}$ into $\hat{w}_i^t$ by

$$\hat{w}_i^t = \begin{cases} \alpha(\text{sign}(w_i)), & |w_i| \geq \Delta \\ 0, & |w_i| < \Delta \end{cases} \quad (1)$$

where $\Delta = \frac{0.7}{n}\|\mathbf{w}\|_1$, $\alpha = \frac{1}{|I|}\sum_{i \in I}|w_i|$, and $I = \{i | w_i \neq 0\}$. α is a scaling factor that is multiplied by ternary values.

For binarization, w_i is binarized into $\hat{w}_i^b$ during inference using the binarization method from (Rastegari et al., 2016) by

$$\hat{w}_i^b = \alpha(\text{sign}(w_i)) \quad (2)$$

where $\alpha = \frac{1}{n}\|\mathbf{w}\|_1$. α is a scaling factor that is multiplied by binary values. The activations x are quantized into $\hat{x}$ using the quantization function

$$\hat{x} = \text{round}((x - x_{min})/s) \cdot s + x_{min}. \quad (3)$$

where $s = (x_{max} - x_{min})/(2^{bitwidth} - 1)$

For training, we calculate the gradient of the distillation loss from Eq. 16 w.r.t the quantized weights and update the full-precision weight of the quantized model. Since the quantization function in Eq 1, 2, and 3 are not differentiable, a straight-through estimator adopted by (Courbariaux et al., 2015) is used to back propagate through the quantization function 1, 2, and/or 3. With this, the gradient $\frac{\partial \hat{x}}{\partial x}$ is approximated as an identity, so $\frac{\partial L}{\partial x}$ can be calculated as

$$\frac{\partial L}{\partial x} = \frac{\partial L}{\partial \hat{x}}\frac{\partial \hat{x}}{\partial x} \quad (4)$$

In our work, we use the knowledge distillation method from (Zhang et al., 2020; Bai et al., 2021) during fine-tuning as shown in Eq. 16. Which parts of the BERT are quantized can be seen on Appendix A.

3 Efficient Two Stage Progressive Quantization Method

With the complex loss landscape of binary/ternary models, training with binary/ternary weights and with quantized activations directly could lead the BERT model to converge to a poor local minimum. Therefore, we use an efficient two-stage progressive quantization (ETSPQ) method. The details of the ETSPQ method are provided in Alg 1. In the first stage, we progressively lower the bitwidth of weights down to binary (or to our desired bitwidth) while fine-tuning it on the target downstream task. The first stage allows us to have a good starting point as we are going to use our binarized/ternarized model weights to then fine-tune the model with quantized activations. In the 2nd stage, with our binarized/ternarized model weights,

Model	W-A	Size (MB)	FLOPs (G)	CoLA	SST2	MRPC	STS-B	QNLI	QQP	MNLI-m	RTE	avg
Full precision	32-32	417.6	22.5	59.9	93.6	87.3	89.6	91.8	91.4	84.7	72.9	83.9
TernaryBERT	2-8	28.0	6.4	55.7	92.8	87.5	87.7	91.5	90.1	83.5	72.2	82.6
ETSPQ w/o aug.	2-8	28.0	6.4	55.4	93.2	87.7	89.3	91.8	**91.4**	**84.8**	74.0	83.1
ETSPQ	2-8	28.0	6.4	**58.8**	**93.9**	**88.0**	**89.8**	**92.0**	**91.4**	**84.8**	**76.9**	**84.5**
BinaryBERT	1-8	16.5	3.1	55.5	93.2	86.0	89.2	**91.6**	91.2	**84.2**	74.0	83.1
ETSPQ	1-8	13.4	3.1	**55.6**	**93.9**	**88.2**	**89.6**	**91.6**	**91.3**	**84.2**	**74.7**	**83.6**
BinaryBERT	1-4	16.5	1.5	53.3	**93.7**	86.0	88.6	**91.4**	**91.2**	**83.9**	71.5	82.6
ETSPQ	1-4	13.4	1.5	**56.2**	93.0	**88.2**	**88.9**	90.6	91.0	83.6	**74.7**	**83.2**

Table 1: Quantization performance for GLUE dev dataset. W-A stands for the bit width of weights and activations.

we then progressively lower the activation bits.

However, to save training time at the same time getting the best possible performance, we choose which bitwidth to finetune on and to initialize from and which bitwidth to fine-tune under augmented data based on the performance of BERT under that bitwidth, unlike (Zhuang et al., 2018).

Algorithm 1: Two-stage progressive quantization

Input: Train/Dev data or Aug train data; 32-bit teacher model; Student model initialized from the teacher model
Output: student model with k-bit weights and p-bit activations

```
/* Progressively reduce bitwidth of weights */
wbits = [32, 8, 2, 1]; abits = [32, 8, 4]
for k in range(1,4) do
    -Initialize the student model weights from a model with wbits[k-1] bit weights
    -Use augmented data if wbits[k] ≤ 2, else use non-augmented data
    for epoch=1,...,max epoch do
        for t=1,...,data size do
            train student and quantize student with wbits[k] bit weights and save the best student model
/* Progressively reduce bitwidth of activations */
for p in range(1,3) do
    -Initialize the student model weights from a model with wbits[k] bit weights and abits[p-1] bit activations
    for epoch=1,...,max epoch do
        for t=1,...,data size do
            train the quantized student model with abits[p] bit activations and wbits[k] bit weights and save the best student model
```

3.1 Selective Bitwidth Finetuning

Rather than progressively quantizing weights/activations i.e., 32-bit→16-bit→8-bit→4-bit→2-bit→1-bit as in (Zhuang et al., 2018) for each stage, we progressively quantizes the weights, i.e., 32-bit→8-bit →2-bit→1-bit, in the first stage, and then the activations, i.e., 32-bit→8-bit→4-bit, in the second stage, as we found that for BERT, the performance doesn't change a lot if we fine-tune for more different bit-widths as shown in Table 2. From (Bai et al., 2021), the performance doesn't drop until weights are ternarized and there is no point in fine-tuning a 16-bit BERT model since an 8-bit BERT model could reach the same performance as the full precision.

Also, the performance barely changes when using a 4-bit BERT model as a starting point versus using a 8-bit BERT model as a starting point when finetuning a 2-bit BERT model, so we just use an 8-bit BERT model as a starting point.

3.2 Selective Data Augmentation

Data augmentation was used on BERT with ≤ 2 bit weights. Applying data augmentation for ≥ 8 bit BERT model is not necessary since the performance doesn't drop w.r.t to the full-precision BERT as shown in Table 5, meaning that it is able to find the optimal point without data augmentation.

4 Experiments

We measure the performance of ETSPQ on GLUE (Wang et al., 2018) and compare ETSPQ with the latest ternarization/binarization methods.

Using the V100 GPU, we fine tune with a batch size of 16 for CoLA, and 32 for other datasets and we use AdamW (Loshchilov and Hutter, 2019) with weight decay of 0.01 and learning rate of 5e-5 with a linear learning rate scheduler for five epochs.

4.1 Results

The GLUE benchmark consists of different natural language tasks. We evaluate the performance on Table 1 on the dev set, using Matthews correlation for CoLA (Warstadt et al., 2019); accuracy for SST2 (Socher et al., 2013), QNLI (Rajpurkar et al., 2016), MNLI (Williams et al., 2018), and RTE (Bentivogli et al., 2009); accuracy for MRPC (Dolan and Brockett, 2005) and QQP (Chen et al.); and, Spearman correlation for STS-B (Cer et al., 2017). Also, the average performance for all dev datasets is reported in the last column of Table 1.

Table 1 shows using our method we can ternarize BERT, compressing it by 14.9x and get a performance greater than or equal to that of the full-precision model on all GLUE development datasets, except for CoLA while using data augmentation and 8-bit activations. ETSPQ method still achieves a better performance on average compared to TernaryBERT even without data augmentation.

With binary weights and 8-bit activations, we outperform BinaryBERT (Bai et al., 2021) on all GLUE development sets. With binary weights and 4-bit activations, our ETSPQ on average outperforms BinaryBERT. At the same time, we get a reduction of 18% w.r.t (Bai et al., 2021) model size because (Bai et al., 2021) has an embedding layer twice the size as BERT embedding layer.

Ternarizing the weights and quantizing the activations to 8 bits allows us to reduce the inference flops by at least 7x while binarizing the weights and quantizing the activations to 4 bits allows us to reduce the flops by 15x. Therefore, 7x and 15x speedup will be gained for inference, respectively on CPU.

4.2 Ablation Studies

In this section, we test the performance of data augmentation under certain bitwidth settings and test the performance of different bit reduction settings. For all different cases, knowledge distillation method from (Zhang et al., 2020) is applied during fine-tuning.

4.2.1 Importance of bit reduction settings

In this section, we test out the performance of certain bit reduction settings, unlike (Zhuang et al., 2018) without using data augmentation. We test these settings on a BERT model with ternary weights and full precision activations with the same hyperparameters as before. For example, "32→2" means fine-tuning the ternary model with the initialization of the full-precision finetuned BERT.

Setting	CoLA	SST2	MRPC	STS-B	QNLI
32→16→8→4→2	55.4	93.2	88.0	89.3	91.9
32→16→8→2	53.4	93.2	87.0	89.1	91.5
32→16→2	53.6	93.1	87.0	89.2	91.4
32→8→4→2	53.7	93.1	88.0	89.3	91.9
32→8→2	55.2	93.2	87.7	89.3	91.8
32→4→2	54.7	93.2	87.7	89.3	91.8
32→2	52.7	92.8	87.0	88.6	91.4

Table 2: Results of different progressive quantization settings

Setting	CoLA	SST2	MRPC	STS-B	QNLI
32→16→8→4→2	50	205	21	36	510
32→16→8→2	40	168	16	29	403
32→16→2	30	125	12	20	303
32→8→4→2	39	170	15	28	405
32→8→2	29	123	12	21	301
32→4→2	30	124	12	20	302
32→2	20	80	8	14	203

Table 3: Runtime for different progressive quantization settings in minutes.

From Table 2, we can see that fine-tuning for more bitwidths doesn't necessarily get us more performance. For example, "32→8→4→2" has almost the same performance as "32→16→8→4→2" with "32→16→8→4→2" outperforming only on CoLA and on SST-2. "32→8→2" also has almost the same performance as "32→16→8→4→2", but "32→8→2" only falls behind on MRPC, CoLA, QNLI by at most 0.3 points.

Therefore, the full-precision model is a good initialization point when fine-tuning an 8 bit model. When the 8 bit model reaches the optimal point, the 8 bit model will also be a good intialization point when fine-tuning a 2 bit model and the resulting 2 bit model will also have a good performance. Therefore, to get the best tradeoff in terms of speed and performance, it is better to use the bit reduction setting, "32→8→2".

4.2.2 Progressively Quantize Weights First or Activations First?

Setting	CoLA	SST2	MRPC	STS-B	QNLI
32→8→2→2+8	55.4	93.2	87.7	89.3	91.8
32→32+8→8+8→2+8	55.3	93.2	87.8	89.0	91.5

Table 4: Performance of progressively reducing weight bitwidth first vs activation bitwidth first.

We also evaluate whether it is better to first progressively reduce the bitwidth of activations or to first progressively reduce the bitwidth of weights while fine-tuning. As seen in Table 4, there is negligible performance drop when trying to first progressively reduce the bitwidth of activations. Results in Table 4 are recorded using a ternary BERT with 8 bit activations, using weight bit reduction settings, "32→8→2".

4.2.3 Importance of selective Data Augmentation

	CoLA		MRPC		SST2	
Weight Bits	-aug	+aug	-aug	+aug	-aug	+aug
16	62.0	61.5	88.1	87.9	93.6	93.8
8	62.3	62.9	88.0	88.0	94.3	94.4
4	59.0	58.5	88.0	88.0	93.9	93.7
2	54.1	58.5	87.7	88.2	93.1	93.9
1	47.2	52.6	84.5	87.3	92.4	93.5

Table 5: Results of data augmentation on different weight bitwidths.

In this section, we evaluate the importance of applying data augmentation under certain bitwidths. This helps us to determine which bitwidth to train with data augmentation to get the best performance which will then be used as initialization point when fine tuning the lower bitwidth model. From Table 5, using data augmentation for an ≥ 8 bit BERT does not improve the performance by a lot as we can see that 8 and 16 bit BERT has almost the same performance. Therefore, data augementation is best when fine-tuning on a ≤ 2 bit BERT.

5 Conclusion

In this work, we introduced an efficient two-stage progressive quantization method to solve the problem of irregular and complex landscape of BERT incurred by the binarization/ternarization of its weights and to reduce the training burden of progressive quantization. We are the first to outperform the state-of-the-art binarization method of BERT model without adding an extra module. Moreover, our ternary BERT can outperform the performance of its full-precision counterpart. Also, we can outperform the state-of-the-art BERT model with ternary weights on almost all GLUE datasets without the use of data augmentation.

References

Haoli Bai, Wei Zhang, Lu Hou, Lifeng Shang, Jin Jin, Xin Jiang, Qun Liu, Michael Lyu, and Irwin King. 2021. BinaryBERT: Pushing the limit of BERT quantization. In *Proceedings of the 59th Annual Meeting of the Association for Computational Linguistics and the 11th International Joint Conference on Natural Language Processing (Volume 1: Long Papers)*, pages 4334–4348, Online. Association for Computational Linguistics.

Luisa Bentivogli, Bernardo Magnini, Ido Dagan, Hoa Trang Dang, and Danilo Giampiccolo. 2009. The fifth PASCAL recognizing textual entailment challenge. In *TAC*.

Daniel Cer, Mona Diab, Eneko Agirre, Iñigo Lopez-Gazpio, and Lucia Specia. 2017. SemEval-2017 task 1: Semantic textual similarity multilingual and crosslingual focused evaluation. In *Proceedings of the 11th International Workshop on Semantic Evaluation (SemEval-2017)*, pages 1–14, Vancouver, Canada. Association for Computational Linguistics.

Zihan Chen, Hongbo Zhang, Xiaoji Zhang, and Leqi Zhao. Quora Question Pairs.

ARM Cortex-M. 2020. https://developer.arm.com/ip-products/processors/cortex-m.

Mattieu Courbariaux, Yoshua Bengio, and Jean-Pierre David. 2015. BinaryConnect: Training Deep Neural Networks with binary weights during propagations.

Jacob Devlin, Ming-Wei Chang, Kenton Lee, and Kristina Toutanova. 2019. BERT: Pre-training of deep bidirectional transformers for language understanding. In *Proceedings of the 2019 Conference of the North American Chapter of the Association for Computational Linguistics: Human Language Technologies, Volume 1 (Long and Short Papers)*, pages 4171–4186, Minneapolis, Minnesota. Association for Computational Linguistics.

William B. Dolan and Chris Brockett. 2005. Automatically constructing a corpus of sentential paraphrases. In *Proceedings of the Third International Workshop on Paraphrasing (IWP2005)*.

Lu Hou, Zhiqi Huang, Lifeng Shang, Xin Jiang, Xiao Chen, and Qun Liu. 2020. Dynabert: Dynamic bert with adaptive width and depth. In *Advances in Neural Information Processing Systems*.

Xiaoqi Jiao, Yichun Yin, Lifeng Shang, Xin Jiang, Xiao Chen, Linlin Li, Fang Wang, and Qun Liu. 2020. TinyBERT: Distilling BERT for natural language understanding. In *Findings of the Association for Computational Linguistics: EMNLP 2020*, pages 4163–4174, Online. Association for Computational Linguistics.

Fengfu Li, Bo Zhang, and Bin Liu. 2016. Ternary Weight Networks.

Ilya Loshchilov and Frank Hutter. 2019. Decoupled weight decay regularization. In *ICLR*.

Haotong Qin, Yifu Ding, Mingyuan Zhang, Qinghua Yan, Aishan Liu, Qingqing Dang, Ziwei Liu, and

Xianglong Liu. 2022. Bibert: Accurate fully binarized bert. In *International Conference on Learning Representations (ICLR)*.

Pranav Rajpurkar, Jian Zhang, Konstantin Lopyrev, and Percy Liang. 2016. SQuAD: 100,000+ questions for machine comprehension of text. In *Proceedings of the 2016 Conference on Empirical Methods in Natural Language Processing*, pages 2383–2392, Austin, Texas. Association for Computational Linguistics.

Mohammad Rastegari, Vicente Ordonez, Joseph Redmon, and Ali Farhadi. 2016. Xnor-net: Imagenet classification using binary convolutional neural networks. In *ECCV*.

Richard Socher, Alex Perelygin, Jean Wu, Jason Chuang, Christopher D. Manning, Andrew Ng, and Christopher Potts. 2013. Recursive deep models for semantic compositionality over a sentiment treebank. In *Proceedings of the 2013 Conference on Empirical Methods in Natural Language Processing*, pages 1631–1642, Seattle, Washington, USA. Association for Computational Linguistics.

Zhiqing Sun, Hongkun Yu, Xiaodan Song, Renjie Liu, Yiming Yang, and Denny Zhou. 2020. MobileBERT: a compact task-agnostic BERT for resource-limited devices. In *Proceedings of the 58th Annual Meeting of the Association for Computational Linguistics*, pages 2158–2170, Online. Association for Computational Linguistics.

Alex Wang, Amanpreet Singh, Julian Michael, Felix Hill, Omer Levy, and Samuel Bowman. 2018. GLUE: A multi-task benchmark and analysis platform for natural language understanding. In *Proceedings of the 2018 EMNLP Workshop BlackboxNLP: Analyzing and Interpreting Neural Networks for NLP*, pages 353–355, Brussels, Belgium. Association for Computational Linguistics.

Alex Warstadt, Amanpreet Singh, and Samuel R. Bowman. 2019. Neural network acceptability judgments. *Transactions of the Association for Computational Linguistics*, 7:625–641.

Adina Williams, Nikita Nangia, and Samuel Bowman. 2018. A broad-coverage challenge corpus for sentence understanding through inference. In *Proceedings of the 2018 Conference of the North American Chapter of the Association for Computational Linguistics: Human Language Technologies, Volume 1 (Long Papers)*, pages 1112–1122, New Orleans, Louisiana. Association for Computational Linguistics.

Ofir Zafrir, Guy Boudoukh, Peter Izsak, and Moshe Wasserblat. 2019. Q8BERT: Quantized 8Bit BERT. *CoRR*, abs/1910.06188.

Wei Zhang, Lu Hou, Yichun Yin, Lifeng Shang, Xiao Chen, Xin Jiang, and Qun Liu. 2020. TernaryBERT: Distillation-aware ultra-low bit BERT. In *Proceedings of the 2020 Conference on Empirical Methods in Natural Language Processing (EMNLP)*, pages 509–521, Online. Association for Computational Linguistics.

Bohan Zhuang, Chunhua Shen, Mingkui Tan, Lingqiao Liu, and Ian Reid. 2018. Towards Effective Low-Bitwidth Convolutional Neural Networks. In *Proceedings of the IEEE Conference on Computer Vision and Pattern Recognition (CVPR)*.

A Bert Quantization:

BERT contains N identical transformer encoder layers with the same architecture but with different parameters. A transformer layer usually contains a Multi-Head Attention (MHA) module and a Feed-Forward Network (FFN) module. Before the input goes through the transformer layers, the input first gets processed at the embedding layer as

$$\mathbf{H}_1 = \text{EM}_{\mathbf{W}^E}(\mathbf{z}) + \text{EM}_{\mathbf{W}^S}(\mathbf{z}) + \text{EM}_{\mathbf{W}^P}(\mathbf{x}) \quad (5)$$

where EM is the embedding function that uses the indices $\mathbf{z}$ to extract the word, segmentation and position embeddings from the $\mathbf{W}^E$, $\mathbf{W}^S$, $\mathbf{W}^P$ lookup tables, respectively. $\mathbf{W}^E$, $\mathbf{W}^S$, $\mathbf{W}^P$ are learnable parameters. Then the output of the embedding layer $\mathbf{H}_1$ becomes the input for the first transformer layer.

In the l-th Transformer layer, the input $\mathbf{H}_l \in \mathbb{R}^{n \times d}$ where n and d are the sequence length and hidden state size, respectively, first goes through the MHA module. In the MHA module with N_H attention heads, the head contains the parameters, $\mathbf{W}_h^Q$, $\mathbf{W}_h^K$, $\mathbf{W}_h^V \in \mathbb{R}^{d \times d_h}$ where $d_h = \frac{d}{N_H}$. Using the dot product of queries and keys from the input, the attention scores are calculated as:

$$\mathbf{A}_h = \mathbf{Q}\mathbf{K}^\top = \mathbf{H}_l \mathbf{W}_h^Q (\mathbf{H}_l \mathbf{W}_h^K)^\top \quad (6)$$

The softmax function is then applied on the attention scores to get the output of each head, head_h as

$$\text{head}_h = \text{Softmax}(\frac{\mathbf{A}_h}{\sqrt{d}})\mathbf{H}_l \mathbf{W}_h^V \quad (7)$$

The output of the multi-head attention is calculated as:

$$\text{MHA}(\mathbf{H}_l) = \text{Concat}(\text{head}_1, ..., \text{head}_{N_H})\mathbf{W}^O \quad (8)$$

A layer normalization is then applied on the output of MHA plus the input of the MHA as shown below

$$\mathbf{X}_l = \text{LN}(\text{MHA}(\mathbf{H}_l) + \mathbf{H}_1) \quad (9)$$

Then the output of that layer-normalization, $\mathbf{X}_l$, is then inputed into the FFN layer which has two linear layers containing the parameters, $\mathbf{W}^{\text{Int}} \in \mathbb{R}^{d \times 4d}$ and $\mathbf{W}^{\text{Out}} \in \mathbb{R}^{4d \times d}$. The output of FFN can be calculated as

$$\text{FFN}(\mathbf{X}_l) = \text{GeLU}(\mathbf{X}_l \mathbf{W}^{\text{Int}} + \mathbf{b}^{\text{Int}})\mathbf{W}^{\text{Out}} + \mathbf{b}^{\text{Out}} \quad (10)$$

Then, a layer normalization is then applied on the output of FFN plus the input of the FFN as shown below

$$\mathbf{H}_{l+1} = \text{LN}(\text{FFN}(\mathbf{X}_l) + \mathbf{X}_1) \quad (11)$$

Following (Zafrir et al., 2019; Zhang et al., 2020; Bai et al., 2021), we quantize the weights $\mathbf{W}^E$ from eq. 5, $\mathbf{W}^Q$, $\mathbf{W}^K$, $\mathbf{W}^V$ from eq. 6 and 7, $\mathbf{W}^O$ from eq. 8, $\mathbf{W}^{\text{Int}}$ and $\mathbf{W}^{\text{Out}}$ from eq. 10 and also quantize the inputs which will be multiplied by these weights. $\mathbf{W}^S$, $\mathbf{W}^P$ and the biases are not quantized as told in (Zhang et al., 2020; Bai et al., 2021), because these parameters' sizes are negligible and operations in the softmax, layer normalization and the task specific layer are kept in full precision because the parameters in these operations are negligible and quantizing them can significantly hurt the performance.

(Zhang et al., 2020) proposed TernaryBERT to ternarize the weights and quantized the activations to 8 bits using layer wise knowledge distilation from (Jiao et al., 2020) to transfer the knowledge of a full precision model to a ternary model by minimizing the mean-squared error (MSE) between the teacher embedding output $\mathbf{H}_1^T$ and the student embedding output $\mathbf{H}_1^S$ as shown in Eq. 12; between the teacher multi-head attention (MHA) scores $\mathbf{A}^T$ and the student MHA output $\mathbf{A}^S$ as shown in Eq. 14; and between teacher feed-forward network (FFN) $\mathbf{H}_l^T$ and the student FFN output $\mathbf{H}_l^S$ as shown in Eq. 13. And by minimizing the soft cross-entropy loss between the student's logit $\mathbf{y}^S$ and the teacher's logit $\mathbf{y}^T$ as shown in Eq. 15.

$$\mathcal{L}_{emb} = \text{MSE}(\mathbf{H}_1^S, \mathbf{H}_1^T) \quad (12)$$

$$\mathcal{L}_{trm} = \sum_{l=1}^{L} \text{MSE}(\mathbf{H}_l^S, \mathbf{H}_l^T) \quad (13)$$

$$\mathcal{L}_{att} = \sum_{l=1}^{L} \text{MSE}(\mathbf{A}_l^S, \mathbf{A}_l^T) \quad (14)$$

$$\mathcal{L}_{pred} = \text{SCE}(\mathbf{y}^S, \mathbf{y}^T) \quad (15)$$

$$\mathcal{L} = \mathcal{L}_{pred} + \mathcal{L}_{emb} + \mathcal{L}_{trm} + \mathcal{L}_{att} \quad (16)$$

Model	W-A	Size (MB)	CoLA	SST2	MRPC	STS-B	QNLI	QQP	MNLI-m	RTE	avg
Full precision	32-32	417.6	51.1	92.8	88.1/83.3	87.0/85.8	90.8	71.2/89.2	84.5	70.2	81.6
TernaryBERT	2-8	28.0	47.8	92.9	87.5/82.6	84.3/82.7	90.0	70.4/88.4	83.0	68.4	80.1
ETSPQ	2-8	28.0	**50.8**	**93.1**	**88.1/83.7**	**86.3/85.2**	**90.9**	**71.4/89.3**	**84.3**	**70.0**	**81.5**
BinaryBERT	1-8	16.5	**51.6**	91.9	85.9	82.3	89.8	89.0	**84.1**	67.3	80.2
ETSPQ	1-8	13.4	50.0	**93.0**	**87.6**	**84.8**	**90.1**	**89.1**	83.9	**67.5**	**80.8**
BinaryBERT	1-4	16.5	**47.9**	**93.1**	86.6	82.9	**89.7**	**89.0**	**83.6**	65.8	79.8
ETSPQ	1-4	13.4	46.9	93.0	**87.0**	**84.5**	89.3	**89.0**	83.5	**68.0**	**80.2**

Table 6: Quantization performance for GLUE test dataset. For binary weights, we only compare accuracy for QQP, F1 for MRPC, and Spearman Correlation for STS-B because in (Bai et al., 2021), results are only represented in these metrics.

Model	W-A	SQuAD2.0
Full precision	32-32	75.2/77.9
TernaryBERT	2-8	73.3/76.6
ETSPQ	2-8	**74.5/77.5**
BinaryBERT	1-8	73.6/76.5
ETSPQ	1-8	**73.9/76.8**
BinaryBERT	1-4	**72.5/75.4**
ETSPQ	1-4	72.1/75.2

Table 7: Our performance vs state of the art methods for SQuAD datasets.

Task	-aug	+aug
CoLA	8.5k	220k
SST2	67k	1135k
MRPC	3.7k	226k
STS-B	5.7k	327k
QNLI	108k	4278k
RTE	2.5k	147k

Table 8: Size of the dataset for each task with and without data augmentation from (Jiao et al., 2020)

Task	-aug	+aug
CoLA	2.2	52
SST2	8.0	129
MRPC	1.1	52
STS-B	1.4	75
QNLI	20	403
RTE	0.6	30

Table 9: Runtime in minutes for one epoch for each task with and without data augmentation from (Jiao et al., 2020)

B GLUE Test Results

On GLUE test set, we can also achieve a comparable performance w.r.t. the full-precision baseline, only losing around 0.1 % of the full precision average performance with ternary weights and 8-bit activations according to Table 6. With binary weights and 8-bit activations, we outperform BinaryBERT (Bai et al., 2021) on all GLUE test set except for MNLI and CoLA.

C SQuAD 2.0 Results

We also perform experiments to measure the performance of ETSPQ on SQuAD 2.0 (Rajpurkar et al., 2016) datasets and compare with state-of-the-art quantized models. From Table 7, using ternary weights we outperform the performance of (Zhang et al., 2020). With binary weights, we can outperform the performance of (Bai et al., 2021) for 8 bit activations, but for 4 bit activations we achieved a comparable performance.

D Further Analysis

In this section, we study the real impact of data augmentation and Two-Stage Progressive Quantization (TSPQ) on the performance of quantized BERT with binary weights and 4-bit activations by plotting the performance on the dev set over the number of iterations for the case "Augmentation" where we use only data augmentation and use the full precision fine-tuned model initialization; for the case "TSPQ" where we use the slightly higher precision quantized fine-tuned model initialization; and for the case "Baseline" where we only use the full precision fine-tuned model initialization.

Fine-tuning with data augmentation for one epoch takes longer and takes more iterations than fine-tuning without data augmentation for five epochs on a GLUE task due to the larger size of the augmented data.

Therefore, the model running with more epochs has more opportunities to adjust its weights properly under the quantization constraint and it is unfair to just compare the effects of using data augmentation for one epoch vs five epochs without data augmentation as previous works did.

As a result of that, we made sure that the quantized model is being fine-tuned for the same num-

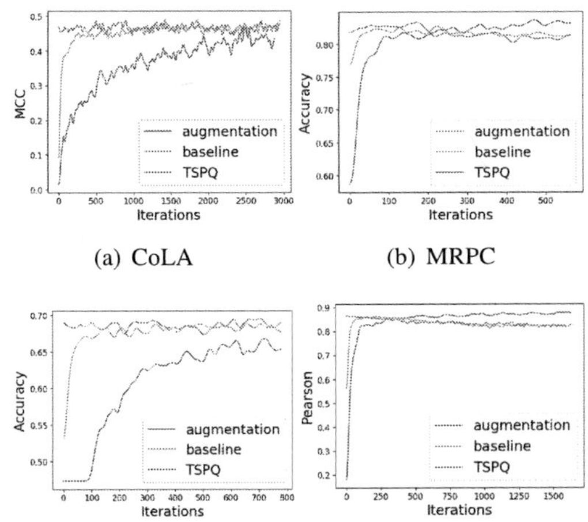

(a) CoLA (b) MRPC (c) RTE (d) STS-B

Figure 2: Performance over training iterations on CoLA (a), MRPC (b), RTE (c), and STS-B (d) on dev set for binary weights and 4 bit activations.

ber of iterations and not necessarily the same number of epochs for all three cases as illustrated in Figure 2. Knowledge distillation from (Zhang et al., 2020) and activation quantization function from Eq. 3 is used in all 3 cases

Figure 2 shows that the use of data augmentation is not beneficial across all datasets unless fine-tuning the model for a large number of iterations. For instance, the performance increase for data augmentation is a lot more progressive for RTE and CoLA datasets. In this case, fine-tuning can be performed for the non-augmented datasets with significantly fewer iterations to reach optimal performance. On the other hand, the use of data augmentation helps to improve the performance of MRPC and STS-B datasets when fine-tuning the model for a larger number of iterations.

Using ETSPQ, we get a good initial performance for the target bit precision, whereas training it normally would need a few more iterations to approximately match the performance. Figure 2 shows that the trajectory of fine-tuning the quantized BERT using ETSPQ is similar to the Baseline at the later iterations and the curve from ETSPQ is generally above or at a equal height as the curve of the Baseline.

E Comparing with BiBERT

Due to limited space, we do not include BiBERT's results into the main results section. Also BiBERT's method deals with the problems of binarizing activations and weights by replacing the softmax function with a boolean function and by replacing the mean square error (MSE) distillation with the direction mismatch distillation (DMD) for the distillation of the attention scores.

Task	DMD	MSE
CoLA	52.1	52.3
SST2	92.8	92.5
MRPC	86.5	87.0
STS-B	88.8	88.6
QNLI	91.4	91.4

Table 10: Performance of using Direction Mismatch Distillation (DMD) versus using Mean Square Error (MSE) Distillation.

However, using a boolean function does not work when the output of the softmax is supposed to be ≥ 1 bit. Therefore, this is also one of the reasons it wasn't included in the main results and we only compare the performance of using DMD with the performance of using MSE distillation in Table 10.

In Table 10, we can see that the performance doesn't change a lot when using DMD compared to using MSE distillation. Results obtained in the table is obtained using the full-precision BERT as the starting point and finetuning a BERT model with ternary weights and 8 bit activations.

KGRefiner: Knowledge Graph Refinement for Improving Accuracy of Translational Link Prediction Methods

Mohammad Javad Saeedizade[1] **Najmeh Torabian**[2] **Behrouz Minae-Bidgol**[1]
[1] School of Computer Engineering, Iran University of Science and Technology, Tehran, Iran
[2] Department of Computer Engineering, Central Tehran Branch, Islamic Azad University, Tehran, Iran
saeedizade74@gmail.com
najmeh.torabian@gmail.com
b_minaei@iust.ac.ir

Abstract

Link Prediction is the task of predicting missing relations between knowledge graph(KG) entities. Recent work in link prediction mainly attempted to adapt a model to increase link prediction accuracy by using more layers in neural network architecture, which heavily rely on computational resources. This paper proposes the refinement of knowledge graphs to perform link prediction operations more accurately using relatively fast translational models. Translational link prediction models have significantly less complexity (faster) than deep learning approaches but are less accurate; this motivated us to improve their accuracy. Our method uses the ontologies of knowledge graphs to add information as auxiliary nodes to the graph. Then, these auxiliary nodes are connected to ordinary nodes of the KG that contain auxiliary information in their hierarchy. Our experiments show that our method can significantly increase the performance of translational link prediction methods in Hit@10, Mean Rank, and Mean Reciprocal Rank, with the same complexity as translational models.

1 Introduction

Knowledge graphs (KGs) represent a set of interconnected descriptions of entities, including objects, events, or concepts. These graphs are structures by which knowledge is captured in the form of triplets. These triplets consist of three parts: head, relation, and tail. The relation (edge) determines the type of relationship between head and tail nodes.

Despite many efforts to build KGs, they are far from completeness. One of the developing fields in completing KGs is link prediction (LP). LP tries to embed entities and relations in a small continuous vector space to predict missing links in KGs. In the last few years, deep learning approaches have significantly outperformed other methods in LP, but this accuracy came at the cost of computational complexity.

Translational LP models, such as TransE (Bordes et al., 2013), TransH (Wang et al., 2014), TransD (Ji et al., 2015), RotatE (Sun et al., 2019b), and HAKE (Zhang et al., 2020), generally use a straightforward function over head and relation vectors to predict the tail based on distance (Rossi et al., 2021) (Wang et al., 2021). One advantage of translational methods over deep learning techniques is that their score function is considerably faster (Sun et al., 2019a). Since these models are less complex and more efficient, we tried to improve only these translational methods in this work.

Ontologies are concepts or properties to describe an object [1]. Wordnet contains hierarchical ontology only for its entities. Some work tried to use ontology components of Wordnet to boost LP models. For example, GrCluster (Ranganathan et al., 2020) treated ontology components as paths. It defined path similarity over entities in Wordnet and slightly improved LP accuracy. Nonetheless, GrCluster only improved WNNH and WN18, which are not standard LP datasets (Dettmers et al., 2018). Additionally, this work is limited to Wordnet.

Freebase (Bollacker et al., 2008) does not have any hierarchical path for its entity. On the other hand, its relations have a path hierarchy to explain edges. SACN (Shang et al., 2019) exploited additional information of FB15k-237 as auxiliary nodes and created FB15k-237-Attr. Nevertheless, it added numerous nodes to the KG, which makes the method for creating FB15k-237-Attr inefficient for more extensive graphs. Likewise, this method can only be applied to Freebase.

Translational LP models, such as TransE, RotatE, or TransD, when trying to learn the relation between Paris and France, neglect that Paris is a city and France is a country. We introduce ontology components as auxiliary nodes. These auxiliary nodes are connected to related entities that

[1] https:en.wikipedia.orgwikiOntology_(information_science)

Proceedings of The Third Workshop on Simple and Efficient Natural Language Processing (SustaiNLP), pages 10 - 16
December 7, 2022

have these components in their hierarchy. For example, we added an extra node "country" to KG and connected it to all the countries in the KG. Our contributions are as follows:

Firstly, we presented a method for refining KGs that have ontology. Our approach adds auxiliary nodes and embeds similar nodes closer in the embedding space, which increases the accuracy of translational link prediction with the same time and space complexity of translational models. **Secondly**, we used state-of-the-art translational models to evaluate our method on two FB15k-237 and WN18RR. The results showed that accuracy in link prediction was significantly increased on H@10, MRR, and MR, especially on WN18RR.

2 Related Work

We divided related work into four categories.

First, translational models, such as TransE (Bordes et al., 2013), TransH (Wang et al., 2014), TransD (Ji et al., 2015), HAKE (Zhang et al., 2020), are distance-based algorithms that use a straightforward operation over head and relation (mainly summation and/or a projection into a secondary space) to measure the distance to the tail entity. Some work has been introduced over these fast translational models to improve their performance by using hierarchical information. TKRL (Xie et al., 2016) used components of hierarchical structure as a transition to transform KG nodes into secondary space and then performed LP. GrCluster (Ranganathan et al., 2020) used path similarity over entities in Wordnet and slightly improved link prediction accuracy. SACN (Shang et al., 2019) proposed FB15k-237_Attr that has external resources as triplets (new nodes and edges) to improve the result.

GrCluster could not improve the WN18RR, and it is limited to KGs that have ontology for their entities. SACN improved FB15k-237 by creating FB15k-237_Attr, but it added many nodes and edges. Nonetheless, the SACN attribute creator could not be applied to WN18RR. TransC (Lv et al., 2018) brought similar entities closer in the embedding space and improved LP in YAGO, but experiment results show no improvements on Wordnet or Freebase. Our work is similar to this category; It is fast and uses translational models as a core. We pushed the limitation of TransC to have a better LP result on Freebase and Wordnet.

Second, mostly deep models adapt an architecture and rarely use anthologies in their main model. For example, ConvE (Dettmers et al., 2018) used 2D convolution, BERT-ResNet (Lovelace et al., 2021) and KG-BERT (Yao et al., 2019) employed BERT, SACN (Shang et al., 2019) utilized WGCN in its architecture. These models are more accurate but computationally costly.

Thirdly, KG refinement is a sub-field of KG enhancement. Refinement can be done by either adding information to the graph or removing incorrect data (Paulheim, 2017). BioKG (Zhao et al., 2020) worked on medical KGs and has tried to provide a method for removing the inaccurate information in these graphs. In this work, like SACN, we added auxiliary nodes to KGs. These nodes are extracted from ontology hierarchy levels of nodes and edges of KGs.

Lastly, some works introduced similarities over entities or relations. For example, HRS (Zhang et al., 2018) presented relation-cluster and sub-relations in the scoring function of translational models. It created sub-relations and relation-clusters based on clustering results of TransE relations; however, it cannot utilize ontology nor improve WN18RR results. For entity similarity, ETE (Moon et al., 2017) considered that if two entities are embedded closely in the embedding space, they are similar and assigned classes to entities based on closeness. Unlike ETE, our hypothesis is that if two entities use the same relation type in the graph or have common elements in their hierarchies, they are related. We exploited these affiliations (share hierarchical components) by connecting ordinary nodes to their auxiliary nodes if a node has the auxiliary node in its ontology components.

The main distinctions between our work and related work are: First, our method works with any KG with ontology, and it does not matter if it has the hierarchical ontology for nodes or edges. Second, it uses translational models; therefore, it has high speed and less time to train these models (see Table 3).

3 KGRefiner

In this work, we propose a method that uses ontology as an auxiliary node, which refines the KG and increases LP accuracy. These auxiliary nodes can be obtained from the edges of KG or its nodes. For example, in FB15k-237, we do this refinement by using hierarchies of relations, and in WN18RR, we use hierarchies of entities. We add repetitive components of hierarchies to KGs as new (auxiliary) nodes. Then, we introduce a few new relations to connect these auxiliary nodes to other KG nodes.

These auxiliary nodes operate like a magnet for similar entities; They drag similar entities (those entities that share ontology components) together in the embedding space. This closeness of similar entities causes the translational models to prioritize their search for a specific place in the embedding space (e.g., searching between countries when asked what country's capital city is Paris, in evaluation). The rest of this section is dedicated to the proof of this assertion.

Translational link prediction methods, such as TransE, create transition property in their embeddings. For example, in TransE, embeddings are made as $\vec{e_s} + \vec{r} \approx \vec{e_o}$. This means the tail entity should be close to the sum of head and relation in embedding space. Let us consider n entities share an ontology component O in their hierarchy. If we add O to the KG and connect the O to those n entities, the following optimization will happen in TransE:

$$\vec{E_1} + \vec{RelatedTo} \approx \vec{O}$$
$$\vec{E_2} + \vec{RelatedTo} \approx \vec{O}$$
$$\ldots$$
$$\vec{E_n} + \vec{RelatedTo} \approx \vec{O}$$

The loss function minimizes the distance between two sides of equations:

$$\begin{aligned} Loss = & ||\vec{E_1} + \vec{RelatedTo} - \vec{O}|| + \\ & ||\vec{E_2} + \vec{RelatedTo} - \vec{O}|| + \\ & \ldots \\ & ||\vec{E_n} + \vec{RelatedTo} - \vec{O}|| \end{aligned}$$

In the implementation, they are optimized batch-wised. Also, assume it uses the L1 norm as a distance measure. Therefore, the batch loss will be:

$$\begin{aligned} Loss &= \sum_{n=1}^{n} Distance(\vec{E_i} + \vec{RelatedTo}, \vec{O}) \\ &= \sum_{n=1}^{n} Distance(\vec{E_i}, \vec{O} - \vec{RelatedTo}) \\ &= \sum_{n=1}^{n} ||\vec{E_i}, \vec{O} - \vec{RelatedTo}||_1 \end{aligned}$$

Since $(\vec{O} - \vec{RelatedTo})$ can be considered constant, all $\vec{E_i}$ will be dragged to where $(\vec{O} - \vec{RelatedTo})$ is located in the embedding space. For example, if we connect all KG countries to an ontology node "country", then all countries will be embedded closer.

3.1 Refinement of FB15k-237

In FB15k-237, graph relations reflect information about entities. For example, in (Paris, national_capital, France), national_capital has hierarchy of "entity → physical_entity → object → location → region → area → center → seat → capital → national_capital". This hierarchy is a relationship between countries and their capitals, and nodes on one side of relationships (e.g. left side of triplet) can be considered similar (e.g. they are countries). Moreover, higher hierarchy levels usually have more abstract information about objects, but the lower ones are more specific. Therefore, we extracted the last three levels of hierarchies from each relation in this KG to use hierarchy components. Then, for each sub-relation (component), we counted the number of their repetitions in the KG training section triplets. Then, we removed those components with less than 100 repetitions to reduce the number of these components; the number 100 is arbitrary. Finally, 285 sub-relations remained, and we added them to the set of entities in this KG (as auxiliary nodes). We defined two new relations, "RelatedTo" and "HasAttribute", to connect these relation-nodes (auxiliary nodes) to the KG entities. For each triplet, if the entity is the triplet's head, we link it to the auxiliary node by "RelatedTo", and if it is the tail of the triplet, we use "HasAttribute" to establish these connections. For example, to

Algorithm 1: Refinement of FB15k-237

```
Input (TrainTriplets, Hierarchies, MinRep. = 100)
  Hierarchies ← LastLevels(Hierarchies, 3)

  Hierarchies ←
    Repetitives(Hierarchies, MinRep)

  NewEdges = []
  for all (h, r, t) in TrainTriplets do
      for all H in Hierarchies do
          NewEdges ←
          NewEdges + (h, HasAttribute, H)

          NewEdges ←
          NewEdges + (t, RelatedTo, H)
  return TrainTriplets + NewEdges
```

refine relation between Paris and France, (Paris, entity → physical_entity → object → location → region → area → center → seat → capital → national_capital, France), "capital" has repetition over 100, so the following triplets were added to the graph:

$$(France, HasAttribute, capital)$$
$$(Paris, RelatedTo, capital)$$

3.2 Refinement of WN18RR

To refine this graph, we use the hierarchy of entities. In Freebase, we used relationships, but relationships do not give us information about entities in Wordnet. France, for example, has a hierarchy of "existence → place → region → region → administrative region → country". This hierarchy gives us good information about France. We extract the last three levels of entities. Among these levels, we hold those with more than an arbitrary number of 50 repetitions among entities to reduce the number of auxiliary nodes. As a result, 207 levels remained. We add these levels as new nodes to the KG training section and connect them to entities that have these components in their hierarchy with a new type of connection "HasAttribute". For example, France and Iran have a "country" in their hierarchical structure. Then, the following triplets were added to the training section of the graph:

$$(France, HasAttribute, country)$$
$$(Iran, HasAttribute, country)$$

Algorithm 2: Refinement of WN18RR

```
Input
(TrainTriplets, Hierarchies, Entities, MinRep. = 50)
  Hierarchies ← LastLevels(Hierarchies, 3)

  Hierarchies ←
    Repetitives(Hierarchies, MinRep)

  NewEdges = []
  for all e in Entities do
      for all H in Hierarchies do
          if H IsComponentOf e then
              NewEdges ← NewEdges +
              (e, HasAttribute, H)

  return TrainTriplets + NewEdges
```

3.3 New Relations

We introduce new edge types to connect auxiliary nodes to the KG to make them distinguishable from original relation types. Since in WN18RR it is only one relation is needed, we introduce "HasAttribute" to say this node has this ontology attribute in its hierarchy. However, in FB15k-237, only edges have ontology components. Therefore, we need to know on which side of the edge an entity is located (head or tail). Therefore, we introduced two new relations: "HasAttribute" and "RelatedTo".

4 Exprement

4.1 Datasets

We evaluated our work on popular benchmarks: FB15k-237 and WN18RR. In addition, we built two other datasets with KGRefiner: FB15k-237-Refined and WN18RR-Refined from those datasets. The details of the datasets are available in appendix in Table 4.

4.2 Baselines

To demonstrate the effectiveness of our models, we compare results with the original translational models TransE (Bordes et al., 2013), TransH (Wang et al., 2014), RotatE (Sun et al., 2019b), and HAKE (Zhang et al., 2020), with fair setting (see Section 4.4 and Appendix A). In addition, we used FB15k-237-Attr (Shang et al., 2019) to compare our work with other data augmentation methods as base models plus attributes.

For WN18RR, GrCluster (Ranganathan et al., 2020) tried to improve link prediction on Wordnet by using hierarchical data using path similarity. Nevertheless, their report did not show improvement in WN18RR.

4.3 Experimental Results

Table 1 and 2 compares the experimental results of our KGRefiner plus translational models and with previously published results. Results in bold font are the best results in the group, and the underlined results denote the best results in the column. KGRefiner with TransH obtains the highest H@10 and MRR on FB15k-237, and also KGRefiner with RotatE reached the best MR and H@10 in WN18RR.

In tables, results of TransE is taken from (Nguyen et al., 2018), TransH from (Zhang et al., 2018). For other rows, we used OpenKE (Han et al., 2018) and original HAKE implementation to get the scores.

Baseline	H@10	MR	MRR
TransE	50.1	3384	**22.6**
TransE + KGRefiner	**53.7**	**1125**	22.2
TransH	42.4	5875	18.6
TransH + KGRefiner	**51.4**	**1534**	**20.8**
HAKE	52.2	4433	**40.0**
HAKE + KGRefiner	**53.8**	**2125**	25.0
RotatE	54.7	4274	**47.3**
RotatE + KGRefiner	**57.0**	**683**	44.8

Table 1: Link prediction results on WN18RR and its refined version.

Baseline	H@10	MR	MRR
TransE	45.6	347	**29.4**
TransE + Attribute	**47.6**	221	28.8
TransE + KGRefiner	47	**203**	29.1
HAKE	**40.8**	282	**23.8**
HAKE + Attribute	38.4	287	21.7
HAKE + KGRefiner	39.0	**267**	21.4
RotatE	**47.4**	**185**	**29.7**
RotatE + Attribute	43.8	218	27.3
RotatE + KGRefiner	43.9	226	27.9
TransH	36.6	311	21.1
TransH + Attribute	47.7	237	28.2
TransH + KGRefiner	**48.9**	**221**	**30.2**

Table 2: Link prediction results on FB15k-237 and its refined version. The "+ Attribute" is the refined version produced by (Shang et al., 2019)

4.4 Speed of Models

The training time of translational models is much less than deep learning approaches such as ConvE, SACN, ConvKB, etc. The complexity of scoring function and neural network layers in their architecture reduces training speed in deep learning methods. Table 3 compares the time that each model needs to be trained for one epoch on FB15k-237. We ran models on Nvidia K80. For fair comparison embedding dimension for all models is 200. It can be observed that the runtime difference between our best result with KGRefiner (TransH + KGRefiner) and BERT-ResNet (Lovelace et al., 2021) for a small dataset FB15k-237 is around 9.6×10^5s. In other words, our method is 100 times faster. In terms of their accuracy (H@10, MRR, MR), BERT-ResNet scores are (0.514, 0.346, 186) but TransH + KGRefiner are (0.489, 0.302, 221). The scores are slightly lower, but speed is uncomparable.
Apart from that, according to table 4, KGRefiner adds triplets to the training section of these KGs. Therefore, it only increases the training time of WN18RR and FB15k-237 by a factor of 2.65 and 2.02, respectively. It does not increase other measurements' complexity because it adds few nodes to the KGs. Consequently, the training cost of the translational models with KGRefiner is still much cheaper than deep learning techniques.

Model	Time to train	Time to train with KGRefiner
TransE [⊕]	2.8×10^2 s	5.6×10^2 s
TransH [⊕]	5.2×10^2s	1×10^3s
TransD [⊕]	5.2×10^2s	1×10^3s
RotatE [⊕]	5×10^2s	1×10^3s
HAKE [⊕]	1.5×10^4s	3×10^4s
ConvE [⊖]	2.7×10^5s	-
ConvKB [⊖]	4×10^4s	-
BERT-ResNet [⊖] (Lovelace et al., 2021)	9.7×10^4s	-

Table 3: Comparison between translational technique and deep learning methods in training time on the small-standard Freebase sub-graph (FB15k-237) . [⊕]: These models are implemented by OpenKE (Han et al., 2018) and [⊖] are produced by their original implementations.

5 Conclusion and Future work

In this work, we propose KGRefiner, a KG refinement method that alleviates the limitations of translational models by capturing additional information in knowledge graph hierarchies. We used hierarchy components as auxiliary nodes. Refined KG comes by connecting these auxiliary nodes to proper entities. Our empirical results show that our KGRefiner outperforms other state-of-the-art translational models and data augmentation methods on WN18RR. Some models' performance improved on FB15k-237 but was not as good as WN18RR. Furthermore, it is the first augmentation method that works with both Wordnet and Freebase, while old methods only perform only on one dataset.

In our work, we had to manually determine the depth cut of hierarchy and minimum repetition for ontology components extraction. In future works, we will automate these two elements, so the model determines each component. Additionally, KGRefiner cannot improve the accuracy of deep learning methods; therefore, another study is needed to enhance deep models by using ontological information.

References

Kurt Bollacker, Colin Evans, Praveen Paritosh, Tim Sturge, and Jamie Taylor. 2008. Freebase: A collaboratively created graph database for structuring human knowledge. In *Proceedings of the 2008 ACM SIGMOD International Conference on Management of Data*, SIGMOD '08, pages 1247–1250, New York, NY, USA. ACM.

Antoine Bordes, Nicolas Usunier, Alberto Garcia-Duran, Jason Weston, and Oksana Yakhnenko. 2013. Translating embeddings for modeling multi-relational data. *Advances in neural information processing systems*, 26.

Tim Dettmers, Minervini Pasquale, Stenetorp Pontus, and Sebastian Riedel. 2018. Convolutional 2d knowledge graph embeddings. In *Proceedings of the 32th AAAI Conference on Artificial Intelligence*, pages 1811–1818.

Xu Han, Shulin Cao, Lv Xin, Yankai Lin, Zhiyuan Liu, Maosong Sun, and Juanzi Li. 2018. Openke: An open toolkit for knowledge embedding. In *Proceedings of EMNLP*.

Guoliang Ji, Shizhu He, Liheng Xu, Kang Liu, and Jun Zhao. 2015. Knowledge graph embedding via dynamic mapping matrix. In *Proceedings of the 53rd annual meeting of the association for computational linguistics and the 7th international joint conference on natural language processing (volume 1: Long papers)*, pages 687–696.

Justin Lovelace, Denis Newman-Griffis, Shikhar Vashishth, Jill Fain Lehman, and Carolyn Rosé. 2021. Robust knowledge graph completion with stacked convolutions and a student re-ranking network. In *Proceedings of the 59th Annual Meeting of the Association for Computational Linguistics and the 11th International Joint Conference on Natural Language Processing (Volume 1: Long Papers)*, pages 1016–1029, Online. Association for Computational Linguistics.

Xin Lv, Lei Hou, Juanzi Li, and Zhiyuan Liu. 2018. Differentiating concepts and instances for knowledge graph embedding. In *Proceedings of the 2018 Conference on Empirical Methods in Natural Language Processing*, pages 1971–1979.

Changsung Moon, Paul Jones, and Nagiza F Samatova. 2017. Learning entity type embeddings for knowledge graph completion. In *Proceedings of the 2017 ACM on conference on information and knowledge management*, pages 2215–2218.

Dai Quoc Nguyen, Tu Dinh Nguyen, Dat Quoc Nguyen, and Dinh Phung. 2018. A novel embedding model for knowledge base completion based on convolutional neural network. In *Proceedings of North American Chapter of the Association for Computational Linguistics*, pages 327–333.

Heiko Paulheim. 2017. Knowledge graph refinement: A survey of approaches and evaluation methods. *Semantic web*, 8(3):489–508.

Varun Ranganathan, Siddharth Suresh, Yash Mathur, Natarajan Subramanyam, and Denilson Barbosa. 2020. Grcluster: a score function to model hierarchy in knowledge graph embeddings. In *Proceedings of the 35th Annual ACM Symposium on Applied Computing*, pages 964–971.

Andrea Rossi, Denilson Barbosa, Donatella Firmani, Antonio Matinata, and Paolo Merialdo. 2021. Knowledge graph embedding for link prediction: A comparative analysis. *ACM Transactions on Knowledge Discovery from Data (TKDD)*, 15(2):1–49.

Chao Shang, Yun Tang, Jing Huang, Jinbo Bi, Xiaodong He, and Bowen Zhou. 2019. End-to-end structure-aware convolutional networks for knowledge base completion. In *Proceedings of the AAAI Conference on Artificial Intelligence*, volume 33, pages 3060–3067.

Zequn Sun, Jiacheng Huang, Wei Hu, Muhao Chen, Lingbing Guo, and Yuzhong Qu. 2019a. Transedge: Translating relation-contextualized embeddings for knowledge graphs. In *International Semantic Web Conference*, pages 612–629. Springer.

Zhiqing Sun, Zhi-Hong Deng, Jian-Yun Nie, and Jian Tang. 2019b. Rotate: Knowledge graph embedding by relational rotation in complex space. In *International Conference on Learning Representations*.

Meihong Wang, Linling Qiu, and Xiaoli Wang. 2021. A survey on knowledge graph embeddings for link prediction. *Symmetry*, 13(3):485.

Zhen Wang, Jianwen Zhang, Jianlin Feng, and Zheng Chen. 2014. Knowledge graph embedding by translating on hyperplanes. In *Proceedings of the Twenty-Eighth AAAI Conference on Artificial Intelligence*, AAAI'14, pages 1112–1119. AAAI Press.

Ruobing Xie, Zhiyuan Liu, Maosong Sun, et al. 2016. Representation learning of knowledge graphs with hierarchical types. In *IJCAI*, volume 2016, pages 2965–2971.

Liang Yao, Chengsheng Mao, and Yuan Luo. 2019. Kg-bert: Bert for knowledge graph completion. *arXiv preprint arXiv:1909.03193*.

Zhanqiu Zhang, Jianyu Cai, Yongdong Zhang, and Jie Wang. 2020. Learning hierarchy-aware knowledge graph embeddings for link prediction. In *Proceedings of the AAAI Conference on Artificial Intelligence*, volume 34, pages 3065–3072.

Zhao Zhang, Fuzhen Zhuang, Meng Qu, Fen Lin, and Qing He. 2018. Knowledge graph embedding with hierarchical relation structure. In *Proceedings of the 2018 Conference on Empirical Methods in Natural Language Processing*, pages 3198–3207.

Sendong Zhao, Bing Qin, Ting Liu, and Fei Wang. 2020. Biomedical knowledge graph refinement with embedding and logic rules. *arXiv preprint arXiv:2012.01031*.

Dataset	FB15k-237	FB15k-237-Refined	WN18RR	WN18RR-Refined	FB15k-237-Attr
Entities	14541	14826	40943	41150	14744
Relations	237	239	11	12	484
Train Edges	272115	550998	86835	230135	350449
Val. Edges	17535	17535	3034	3034	17535
Test Edges	20466	20466	3134	3134	20466

Table 4: Statistics of the experimental datasets. The refined version represents that graph has some auxiliary nodes. These auxiliary nodes are extracted from entities hierarchy in the original knowledge graph.

A Hyperparameter Settings

We employed the implementation of baselines by OpenKE (Han et al., 2018), and HAKE (Zhang et al., 2020) to produce the result.

To have a fair comparison between translational models, we used an embedding dimension of 200 for all models (to produce the same result as in their paper, some models need more than 1000 dimensions for entity embedding). Also, we removed self adversarial negative sampling from TransE, RotatE, and HAKE and replaced it with typical negative sampling. Moreover, we tried {200, 500, 1000, 2000} epochs, and we picked the best one according to MRR on the validation set for final comparison. Other hyperparameters of the models are those mentioned in OpenKE and HAKE. Hyperparameters for FB15k-237 and FB15k-237-Refined and also WN18RR and WN18RR-Refined are the same. Interestingly, HAKE heavily relied on 1000 embedding dimensions to reproduce the result on its paper.

B Limitations

KGRefiner needs a KG that has ontology for either its nodes or edges. Therefore, in other developing KGs, KGRefiner cannot be applied. In addition, since it brings similar entities closer, this can only improve distance-based models (translational).

Algorithmic Diversity and Tiny Models: Comparing Binary Networks and the Fruit Fly Algorithm on Document Representation Tasks

Tanise Ceron * △ **Nhut Truong** * □ **Aurelie Herbelot** * □O

△ Institute for Natural Language Processing, University of Stuttgart, Germany
□ Center for Mind/Brain Sciences, University of Trento, Italy
O Department of Information Engineering and Computer Science, University of Trento, Italy
tanise.ceron@ims.uni-stuttgart.de,
{leminhnhut.truong,aurelie.herbelot}@unitn.it

Abstract

Neural language models have seen a dramatic increase in size in the last years. While many still advocate that 'bigger is better', work in model distillation has shown that the number of parameters used by very large networks is actually more than what is required for state-of-the-art performance. This prompts an obvious question: can we build smaller models from scratch, rather than going through the inefficient process of training at scale and subsequently reducing model size? In this paper, we investigate the behaviour of a biologically inspired algorithm, based on the fruit fly's olfactory system. This algorithm has shown good performance in the past on the task of learning word embeddings. We now put it to the test on the task of semantic hashing. Specifically, we compare the fruit fly to a standard binary network on the task of generating locality-sensitive hashes for text documents, measuring both task performance and energy consumption. Our results indicate that the two algorithms have complementary strengths while showing similar electricity usage.

1 Introduction

In 2022, the vast majority of state-of-the-art NLP systems are implemented as deep neural models, that is, neural networks with complex architectures which can contain hundreds of billions of parameters. Such models have become so expensive to train that most institutions cannot afford anymore to generate them from scratch. They have also been shown to generate non-negligible amounts of CO_2 emissions (Strubell et al., 2019).

An active research area focuses on model distillation (e.g. Sanh et al., 2019), that is, the process of pruning pretrained large models to only retain the weights truly essential to the system's performance. The result of distillation is a much smaller architecture, faster to run, and less memory-hungry. However, training a large model to then reduce its size seems to be a waste of resources. Ideally, we would make the right design choices to directly implement a model with a reasonable number of parameters. With this goal in mind, the present paper looks at a biologically-inspired architecture which have shown potential as a 'small model' for language processing: The Fruit Fly Algorithm (FFA).

The FFA is inspired by the olfactory system of the fruit fly, *Drosophila melanogaster*. It algorithmically describes how the fly encodes smells in its environment into a binary pattern of activations, using just two layers of neurons. The usefulness of the biological algorithm for computer science was first noted by Dasgupta et al. (2017), who modeled the mechanism as a kind of local-sensitivity hashing relying on random projections, and used it to hash pre-trained document and image vectors. Preissner and Herbelot (2019, 2020) ported the original algorithm to a Natural Language Processing setting and made the fly learn word embeddings. Liang et al. (2021) also applied the FFA to the task of creating word embeddings, serving downstream tasks such as word-sense disambiguation and document classification.

The FFA produces word embeddings of a quality comparable to that of traditional, classic methods such as GLOVE (Pennington et al., 2014) and Word2Vec (Mikolov et al., 2013). While it lags behind the performance of large language models like BERT (Devlin et al., 2019), it consumes only a fraction of inference time as well as computing power (Liang et al., 2021). Moreover, the FFA is an explainable model, thanks to a shallow architecture and sparse, binary feature representations. Taken together, these features promise to alleviate the drawbacks of mainstream giant language models, such as the need for expensive computing resources, environmental concerns and lack of interpretability.

In our work, we aim to take the FFA one step

*Equal contribution

Proceedings of The Third Workshop on Simple and Efficient Natural Language Processing (SustaiNLP), pages 17 - 28
December 7, 2022 ©2022 Association for Computational Linguistics

further and use it to perform **semantic hashing**, that is, the task of learning locality-sensitive, binary vectors for various types of text input. In the general area of computational efficiency, semantic hashing is an extremely useful task: it generates meaningful vector representations at a low number of bits (typically between 8 and 128). The produced hashes can be stored very efficiently and similarity computations can be performed extremely fast over them, using hamming distance.

In the present paper, we provide a comparison of the FFA with another efficient hashing algorithm, namely the Binary Neural Network (BNN) (Hubara et al., 2016). Both techniques are very different in terms of architecture and training regime. In the spirit of increasing 'algorithmic diversity' (Preissner and Herbelot, 2020), we think it worthwhile to investigate the respective benefits of the two methods, and we pitch them against each other on the tasks of document classification and information retrieval. Our results show that the two techniques are complementary in strength while both satisfying requirements of energy efficiency.

2 Related work

Semantic hashing The task of semantic hashing comes from the area of information retrieval, where it is crucial to be able to cluster documents according to their semantic similarity, in order to retrieve documents given a query. One way of going about this problem is to assign a code, hash or vector representation to each document. The more similar the hash of two given documents, the more semantically related they are. These representations should be storable in a fixed number of bits so that the retrieval of documents – through hamming distance – is fast and computationally efficient.

Models for semantic hashing vary, from very simple methods involving counts or tf-idf values (Salton and Michael, 1986), to more complex ones involving deep learning. The current unsupervised state-of-the-art systems rely on heavy machinery such as generative models with variational autoencoders (Chaidaroon and Fang, 2017; Zhang and Zhu, 2019; Hansen et al., 2020), which are capable of reducing the high-dimensional data into a low latent space.

Document classification The task of document classification is a traditional one in NLP, and like many other tasks, it has become associated with more and more complex architectures. A few years ago, classification used to be tackled using different architectures of neural network such as CNNs (Liu et al., 2017) and biLSTMs (Adhikari et al., 2019b) with static word embeddings. Nowadays, the preferred method is to input the entire document into a large language model (LLM), retrieve its representation, and feed it into a fully connected layer or a linear classifier. LLMs are based on Transformers and have a massive amount of parameters, (e.g. 170 billion in GPT-3: Brown et al., 2020). They have fostered substantial progress in search engines in the last few years[1] and indeed create excellent text representations. But they also have the many pitfalls mentioned in our introduction, from low interpretability to high computational cost, as well as erroneous filtering of content in the pretraining process, disfavouring minority groups (Dodge et al., 2021; Bender et al., 2021).

From a purely engineering point of view, the drawbacks of LLMs have prompted the publication of various papers trying to tackle core issues in the models. For instance, Adhikari et al. (2019a) implement knowledge distillation as compression technique in the BERT-large model to deal with the problem of run-time memory caused by these large systems. Another known issue is that standard LLMs such as BERT (Devlin et al., 2019) can only take up to 512 tokens input due to their self-attention mechanisms. Therefore, dealing with long documents can still be a challenge. Researchers have dealt with it by creating Transformer-based models that can take even longer texts as input (Beltagy et al., 2020).

Our own stance is that, beside improving LLMs, our community should experiment with more diverse computational architectures to solve the outstanding problems. As Bender et al. (2021) point out, we should be careful not to focus only on state-of-the-art architectures and encourage instead research efforts and funding into diversifying natural language processing models.

3 Datasets

Six datasets were used to evaluate our algorithms: 20 Newsgroups[2] (20news) (Lang, 2008), Agnews[3]

[1] https://blog.google/products/search/search-language-understanding-bert/

[2] qwone.com/~jason/20Newsgroups/20news-bydate.tar.gz

[3] groups.di.unipi.it/~gulli/AG_corpus_of_news_articles.html

(Zhang et al., 2015), Reuters[4] (Lewis, 1997), TMC[5] (Oza, 2010), Wikipedia (Wiki), and Web of Science[6] (WoS) (Kowsari et al., 2017). Statistics and short descriptions of all datasets can be found in Table 1.

All datasets are available to download, except Wiki, which we collected by scraping English Wikipedia pages. For the 20news dataset, we used the specific version sorted by date. For Reuters, we used the version ModApte R(90). For WoS, we used the medium-size version. Three datasets (20news, Agnews, and Reuters) had already been provided separate train and test sets. Thus we kept these test sets intact for the purpose of comparison, and further split the train sets to extract validation sets.

3.1 Pre-processing

All datasets are lowercased and tokenized with a SentencePiece[7] model, generated from the train split. Using this tokenization method makes our system ready to be used with languages other than English. SentencePiece transforms the data into tokens belonging to a vocabulary of d wordpieces, with d set here at $10,000$. It also returns the log-probabilities of each token in the training data. We will write l_i to refer to the log-probability of token i in the SentencePiece model.

After this initial pre-processing, each dataset is vectorized. For a dataset of n documents, we obtain a matrix of size $n \times d$, where each row represents a document and each column a token in our vocabulary of word pieces. Each cell in the matrix shows the normalized frequency of a token in the document, reweighted by l_i^p, where p is an exponent used to increase or decrease the effect of l_i. The reason for weighing frequencies in this way, rather than using a conventional measure such as tf-idf, is that it allows the system to be incremental at test stage. That is, any new document seen by the model can be vectorized without needing access to the entire document collection.

Finally, we experiment with keeping only the top t words in each (reweighted) document vector, which lets us optimize the number of infrequent and/or uncharacteristic words seen by the system. That is, before feeding the input to the system, we zero out the $d - t$ cells with lowest weights in each row of the matrix.

[4]Downloaded from nltk library.

[5]`catalog.data.gov/dataset/siam-2007-text-mining-competition-dataset`

[6]`data.mendeley.com/datasets/9rw3vkcfy4/6` under the license CC BY 4.0

[7]`https://github.com/google/sentencepiece`

4 Models

4.1 The Binary Neural Network (BNN)

BNN (Hubara et al., 2016) is an example of a light and efficient model, which bridges the gap between production in industry and research. Thus, the model provides an ideal comparison for our FFA. BNNs have a reduced cost of computation with respect to continuous neural networks because weights and activations are binarized at run-time, as well as during gradient computation, with +1 and -1 values. Weights and activations undergo a deterministic binarization step:

$$x^b = Sign(x) = \begin{cases} +1 & \text{if } x \geq 0, \\ -1 & \text{otherwise} \end{cases}$$

where x is the continuous variable and x^b is the binarized value. The Stochastic Gradient Descent, however, is computed with the accumulated continuous-valued weights in order to have high precision.

Our BNN has one input layer, one hidden layer and one output layer. It is trained to predict which class(es) a certain document belongs to. The input is a matrix $R^{n \times d}$ with the pre-processed documents (cf. 3.1) where n is the number of documents in the batch and d is 10,000. The output layer is a binary vector representation of dimensionality $R^{h \times l}$ where h is the number of neurons in the hidden layer and l is the number of labels in the dataset. Cross Entropy loss is computed for single label documents whereas in the multilabel classification the loss combines a sigmoid layer and Binary Cross Entropy.

We experiment with three sizes of hidden layers (32, 64 and 128) and two different learning rates (0.01 and 0.001). The training batch size is kept at 32 across datasets. Training is run for 50 epochs with early stopping after 5 epochs. The number of epochs of each final model varies between 6 and 42.

While the BNN is trained on a classification task, it can also be used for semantic hashing. To get an unseen document's hash, we feed it into the neural network and extract the hidden layer before the classification layer as the representation of the

Dataset	Multi-class	Classes	Num docs	Train-val-test split (%)	Topics
20news	No	20	18846	42-18-40	Newsgroups, such as motorcycles, computer, politics, etc
Agnews	No	4	127600	75-19-6	News articles about the world, sports, business, and science/tech
Reuters	Yes	90	10788	56-16-28	News articles on various topics, such as jobs, gas, housing, wheat, etc
TMC	Yes	22	28596	60-15-25	Air traffic reports
Wiki	No	15	29924	60-20-20	Wikipedia pages in categories, such as music, football, law, etc
WoS	No	35	11967	60-20-20	Scientific papers' abstracts in different fields, such as biochemistry, psychology, etc

Table 1: Statistics and description of datasets

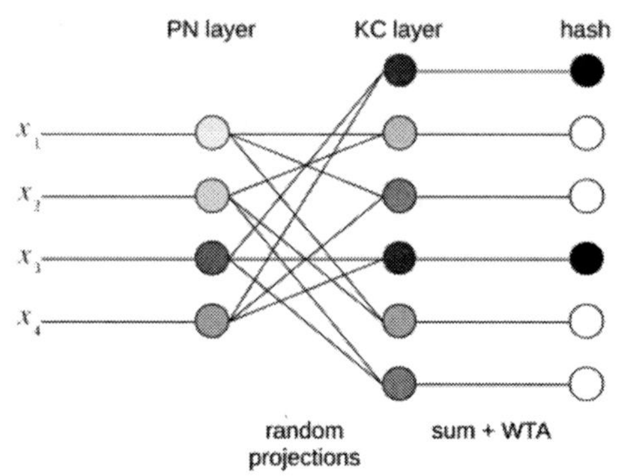

Figure 1: FFA architecture (figure adapted from Preissner and Herbelot (2020).

document. Since the activations of the hidden layer are already binarized, the representation naturally implements binary hashing.

4.2 The Fruit Fly Algorithm (FFA)

The Fruit Fly Algorithm (FFA) takes inspiration from the fruit fly's olfactory system. Specifically, the fruit fly's brain is composed of sparse connections between only two layers of neurons which can assign binary activations to a particular smell (defined as a combination of different types of chemicals). These patterns of activations allow the fruit fly to 'conceptualise' the environment and react to new smells by comparing them to previous smells the fly has been exposed to. Dasgupta et al. (2017) first proposed an implementation of FFA to hash existing pretrained embeddings. In our work, we extend the FFA to learn binary document embeddings from scratch, with low energy consumption.

Following the implementation of (Dasgupta et al., 2017), the FFA model consists of a small feedforward architecture which transforms a document to a binary vector to represent the hash of the document (Fig 1). The input layer, the *projection neuron layer* or *PN layer*, is a vector of d elements $\{x_1...x_d\}$, generated by the vectorization process described in §3.1. Next, this input layer is multiplied by a random projection matrix to form the input to the second layer. The second layer, (*Kenyon Cell layer* or *KC layer*), is represented as a vector of k elements $\{y_1...y_k\}$, which is *larger* than the PN layer ($k >> d$) and is kept at fixed size. The projection matrix is sparse, that is, PN and KC layers are not fully connected. Each KC is connected with a constant number i of nodes in the PN layer, and these connections are randomly allocated at initialization time. The activation value of each KC cell is then simply the sum of i activations from the PN layer. Note that although these connections are uniformly distributed, certain allocations will result in better performance. Finally, hashing is done by a winner-takes-all (WTA) function that sorts the activations in the KC layer, then takes only a small percentage of the most activated values to produce a compact representation of the document. Specifically, $WTA(y_i) = 1$ if y_i is one of the k top values in y and 0 otherwise.

Moreover, we include a Locality Sensitive Hashing (LSH) algorithm as a simple baseline. It is a vanilla random projection method with one non-binary weight matrix, followed by a binarization step to achieve hash values. Random projection LSH is similar to FFA, as the two are from the random projection group of algorithms.

5 BNN and FFA comparison

Our two algorithms have many differences, from their architecture to their optimization regime. We will highlight those differences here to make our experimental results more interpretable.

First, the BNN is a supervised method while

the FFA is in essence unsupervised. This means that when training and optimizing the BNN, we are looking for the best network weights *and* ideal hyperparameters (for both pre-processing and training regime). In contrast, the FFA does not require training of weights, since the projections are random, but still requires hyperparameter setting (including pre-processing and fly-specific features such as the number of random projections per KC or the WTA rate). Note that the BNN uses backpropagation while the FFA only performs forward propagation.

Second, the BNN's natural training grounds is the classification task, which allows us to use a straightforward and efficient objective function. The FFA being unsupervised, it can be optimized on any task that can make direct use of its binary embeddings. In practice, we found that optimizing the FFA's hyperparameters on *Prec@k* gave us better performance than the classification task, so the results we report are based on this choice.

Finally, we should note that the task of this paper, learning binary representations at low-dimensionality, is a natural setting for the BNN but actually challenges the FFA. The strength of the FFA is the massive expansion in dimensionality at the level of the KC layer. Through this mechanism, an actual fruit fly transforms a perceptual input in 50 dimensions into a conceptual representation contained in 2000 neurons. That 40-fold expansion in dimensionality allows the fly to capture many latent features of the perceptual data, some of which, presumably, end up being useful for classification.[8] But our task requires instead that the document features be compressed in at most 128 dimensions (down from 10,000 in input). As we will see later, this will necessitate some adjustments to the original FFA.

5.1 Evaluation

Classification Classification is simply the process of predicting a class for a given document. The accuracy for multi-label and single-label documents is computed as the sum of all true positives and negatives divided by the sum of all true and false positives and negatives from the dataset.

Prec@k Precision at k is a typical information retrieval task. Given some document representation v, the k nearest neighbours of v are computed. Precision is then given as the number of nearest neighbours that have the same class as v, divided by k. All datasets are evaluated with a k value of 100. In the case of multi-label documents, the precision is counted as correct if at least one of the labels is retrieved.

Carbon footprint Aside from task performance, we also measure how the algorithms compare in terms of energy use. For each system, and for each dataset, we compute electricity use in kWh. Since optimization happens differently in the BNN and the FFA, and involves different numbers of hyperparameters, we report the average consumption of a single run (one given set of hyperparameters) for each architecture. In order to show the environmental advantage of the BNN and FFA algorithms, we also report the consumption of a pretrained BERT model for comparison. We use the *CodeCarbon* library (Schmidt et al., 2021) to measure the electricity consumption.

6 Experimental Design

We implement a BNN and an FFA[9] with the aim of generating document hashes at 32, 64 and 128 bits. To evaluate the respective strengths of the two systems, we compare the two architectures according to the two methods described above: precision at k (*prec@k*) and classification (*acc*).

Further, we divide our evaluation of the FFA into three different settings, to investigate how the relation between the dimensionality of the input of the size of the KC layer affects results. Recall that the original FFA expects an expansion in dimensionality which is undesirable from the point of view of the task at hand, where we seek to obtain 32-64-128 bits hashes. To alleviate this issue, we attempt to combine the original architecture with a dimensionality reduction step implemented as Principle Component Analysis (PCA). We apply this step in two different conditions. In the first one (subsequently referred to as PCA+FFA), we apply PCA to the input matrix and feed the first c principal components to the FFA, where c is a hyperparameter to optimize. In the second one (FFA+PCA), we apply PCA 'inside' the FFA, just before the WTA step, in effect reducing the size of the KC layer. As control condition, we also show the results of the original FFA without intervention (henceforth 'Raw FFA').

[8] In that sense, one might argue that the natural fruit fly implements the kind of 'wastefulness' we criticised in Large Language Models – but only across two partially connected layers, and without backpropagation.

[9] Our code is freely available at `https://github.com/minimalparts/SemanticHashingFFA`.

Bits	Eval mode	BNN	LSH	Raw FFA	PCA + FFA	FFA + PCA
32	pre@k	**0.31**	0.08	0.25	0.30	0.25
	acc	0.45	0.17	0.38	0.45	**0.48**
64	pre@k	0.31	0.09	0.25	**0.35**	0.29
	acc	0.48	0.25	0.41	0.55	**0.56**
128	pre@k	0.32	0.11	0.27	**0.39**	0.29
	acc	0.54	0.38	0.48	**0.61**	0.59

Table 2: Results for 20news dataset

Bits	Eval mode	BNN	LSH	Raw FFA	PCA + FFA	FFA + PCA
32	pre@k	**0.79**	0.27	0.31	0.62	0.62
	acc	0.75	0.33	0.42	0.73	**0.78**
64	pre@k	**0.80**	0.27	0.64	0.69	0.59
	acc	**0.81**	0.37	0.43	0.80	0.80
128	pre@k	**0.80**	0.28	0.67	0.72	0.54
	acc	**0.86**	0.41	0.45	0.84	0.80

Table 3: Results for Agnews dataset

Bits	Eval mode	BNN	LSH	Raw FFA	PCA + FFA	FFA + PCA
32	pre@k	**0.61**	0.25	0.50	0.58	0.54
	acc	**0.99**	0.45	0.49	0.62	0.56
64	pre@k	**0.68**	0.27	0.50	0.64	0.54
	acc	**0.99**	0.58	0.48	0.66	0.59
128	pre@k	**0.70**	0.29	0.49	0.66	0.50
	acc	**0.99**	0.74	0.50	0.68	0.61

Table 4: Results for Reuters dataset

Bits	Eval mode	BNN	LSH	Raw FFA	PCA + FFA	FFA + PCA
32	pre@k	0.53	0.24	0.41	0.56	**0.58**
	acc	**0.89**	0.42	0.06	0.19	0.20
64	pre@k	0.58	0.24	0.4	**0.61**	0.56
	acc	**0.91**	0.43	0.11	0.22	0.20
128	pre@k	0.59	0.25	0.43	**0.64**	0.53
	acc	**0.91**	0.46	0.14	0.25	0.21

Table 5: Results for TMC dataset

Bits	Eval mode	BNN	LSH	Raw FFA	PCA + FFA	FFA + PCA
32	pre@k	**0.67**	0.14	0.19	0.55	0.43
	acc	**0.82**	0.33	0.34	0.73	0.70
64	pre@k	**0.70**	0.18	0.21	0.63	0.45
	acc	**0.84**	0.46	0.43	0.81	0.79
128	pre@k	**0.69**	0.24	0.27	0.68	0.40
	acc	0.85	0.62	0.54	**0.86**	0.81

Table 6: Results for Wiki dataset

Bits	Eval mode	BNN	LSH	Raw FFA	PCA + FFA	FFA + PCA
32	pre@k	0.20	0.07	0.27	**0.35**	0.15
	acc	0.51	0.22	0.45	**0.58**	0.46
64	pre@k	0.22	0.09	0.28	**0.37**	0.14
	acc	0.56	0.35	0.46	**0.64**	0.51
128	pre@k	0.22	0.10	0.26	**0.40**	0.13
	acc	0.58	0.60	0.50	**0.71**	0.54

Table 7: Results for WoS dataset

To perform classification with the FFA representations, we feed a simple Logistic Regression[10] model with the documents' hashes, as generated by the fly, and perform one-vs-rest classification.

For all settings, we tune the values of the two hyperparameters of the pre-processing stage: the log-probability exponent p and the number t of top words considered for each document (see §3.1). For the BNN, we also investigate the learning rate of the network. For the FFA, we tune the projection size and WTA rate, as well as the number of principal components retained from the PCA, wherever applicable. For the LSH, there is no tuning.

Since the FFA generates random projections for each fly it creates, we run it 10 times for each combination of dataset and hyperparameters, and select the instance with the best performance on the train set. (Recall that the FFA is unsupervised, so we simply compute *Prec@k* on the n documents seen in training.) We also run 10 times for LSH and average the results. All results reported in §7 are for the best models obtained from the optimization process.

7 Results

7.1 Task performance

Our results are reported in Tables 2 to 8. We provide the best hyperparameter sets in the appendix, for reproducibility purposes. It emerges that the BNN and the FFA complement each other, with one or the other algorithm taking the lead in particular combinations of datasets and tasks. We summarize the main trends in our results below, starting with a description of each experimental setting individually and then highlighting their respective strengths.

BNN baseline: The BNN performs generally very well on the classification task, which is to be expected since it is specifically optimized for that task. It reaches accuracies over 90% on Reuters and

[10]Implementation from scikit-learn: `https://scikit-learn.org/stable/modules/generated/sklearn.linear_model.LogisticRegression.html`.

TMC, at all hash sizes. At 128 bits, it also achieves over 85% for Agnews and Wiki. Its performance is somewhat more disappointing on 20news and WoS (54% and 58% respectively). The results on *prec@k* are more variegated and, interestingly, do not fully follow the classification patterns. The best performance is on Agnews (around 0.8) followed by Reuters and Wiki (around 0.7 at 64 and 128 bits). TMC only reaches 0.59 while the performance on 20news and Wos is again lower (around 0.3 and 0.2 respectively).

Raw FFA: Results with the raw FFA are consistently low, although this setting surprisingly outperforms the BNN on WoS against the *prec@k* measure. This result is not entirely surprising, as the natural fly has a dramatic expansion factor of 40, projecting 50 PN neurons to 2000 KC cells. In our setting, conversely, the PNs get projected onto a *lower* number of KCs.

FFA with PCA postprocessing: Integrating a PCA dimensionality reduction step within the FFA, just before the WTA function, only occasionally improves performance. In some cases, it actually degrades the score of the Raw FFA.

FFA with PCA preprocessing: Out of all FFA settings, this is the one with the best performance. For classification, it does best on Wiki (86%) and WoS (71%), followed by Reuters (68%) and 20news (61%). For *prec@k*, the best results are obtained on Wiki, Reuters and TMC (0.68, 0.66 and 0.64 at 128 bits), followed by 20news and WoS (around 0.40).

LSH: It gets lowest scores for all datasets because it is the simplest algorithm, which serves as a good sanity check.

When comparing both algorithms, we see that for classification, PCA+FFA clearly outperforms the BNN on 20news and WoS, while very much failing to encode TMC and lagging behind on Reuters. Performance is comparable on the Wiki dataset and Agnews. As far as *prec@k* is concerned, PCA+FFA outperforms the BNN again on 20news and WoS, as well as TMC. The two algorithms have more comparable results on Reuters and Wiki, especially at higher hash sizes. The BNN obtains the highest results on Agnews.

7.2 Energy consumption

Table 9 shows energy consumption for the BNN and the PCA+FFA model, measured on a 32-core Linux machine using CPUs only (model AMD Opteron(TM) Processor 6272), with 32GB RAM. For comparison purposes, we also report the consumption of a fine-tuning procedure over a pre-trained BERT model, for the classification task. It is run parallel on a 4 x Nvidia GeForce GTX 1080 Ti, 12 GB. The table reports average figures for single optimization steps with an intuitive measure of electricity usage, by showing how many minutes one could run a single 40W light bulb for the same consumption. The results concerning the exact kWh consumption can be found in Table 1 of appendix A.1. While for the FFA, we give results for the overall consumption as well as a breakdown showing the individual demands of the PCA and the actual fruit fly, the results for BERT represent the fine-tuning of the model run once with the same hyperparameters across datasets [11]. Note that the values of consumption for BERT in the table only consider the fine-tuning of the model for the classification task, refer to Strubell et al. (2019) for more information about the pre-training consumption.

8 Discussion

8.1 Task performance

We first remark that as far as classification is concerned, it is possible to obtain high accuracies on nearly all datasets with at least one of our two lightweight algorithms: results at 128 bits range from 80% to 99% for Agnews, Reuters, TMC and Wiki. The more 'difficult' datasets are 20news and WoS, and interestingly, those are the ones where the FFA outperforms the BNN. As far as *prec@k* is concerned, a very similar picture emerges. Agnews, Reuters, TMC and Wiki reach between 0.69 and 0.80 precision, while 20news and WoS lag behind. Here again, the FFA outperforms the BNN by a very substantial margin.

One notable aspect of our results is that performance in classification does not necessarily transfer to *prec@k*, and vice-versa. The BNN achieves good classification accuracies on TMC but rather low prec@k, while the FFA behaves in exactly the opposite manner. Further, results vary widely depending on datasets, with the BNN and the FFA respectively leading the game on Reuters and WoS for both performance metrics. This seems to indicate that particular data distributions might be

[11] lr=3e-05, seed=42, number of training epochs=3, maximum sequence length=512, batch size for training and validating=8

	Similarity search				Classification			
dataset	**prec@100**	**KC size**	**proj size**	**WTA**	**Acc.**	**KC size**	**proj size**	**WTA**
20news	0.12	14896	10	45	0.69	14239	2	100
agnews	0.32	14885	10	80	0.91	9106	2	100
reuters	0.48	4462	10	62	0.73	14033	2	100
tmc	0.46	14866	10	94	0.22	8233	2	57
wiki	0.24	13848	10	35	0.92	14336	2	100
wos	0.15	2337	7	3	0.82	11236	2	100

Table 8: Bayesian Optimization on the raw FFA, with (nearly) unlimited KCs.

dataset	LSH	BNN	PCA+Fly = FFA (Overall)	BERT	Diff. BERT
20news	19	13	2+18 = 20	548	31x
agnews	34	41	87+81 $\approx$ 169	20153	247x
reuters	8	27	1+7 = 8	288	7x
tmc	18	16	4+16 = 20	1076	25x
wiki	31	21	6+22 $\approx$ 27	1281	48x
wos	11	11	1+9 $\approx$ 11	320	12x

Table 9: Energy consumption of the models in minutes run in a 40W lightbulb (more info about the kWh consumption in appendix A.1). Figures represent one complete run of the models with one pre-determined set of hyperparameters. Values in red and green are the models spending the most and least energy respectively. *Diff. BERT* represents the number of times BERT consumes more over the avg. of all tiny models.

better captured by one or the other algorithm.

Unlike the BNN, the FFA demonstrates a consistent improvement as the hash size increases. This is not surprising, as we mentioned earlier that the FFA is in some sense designed to work at high dimensionality. We investigated this effect further and performed Bayesian Optimization[12] on the FFA's hyperparameters, this time allowing the size of the KC layer to grow up to 15,000 bits. Results are shown in Table 8. Against expectation, a higher KC size does not necessarily translate into better *prec@k*. And while the higher size does make a substantial difference to the classification task, we note that this is obtained with very low projection sizes, meaning that the algorithm reverts to looking at single words in the output.

An inspection into the hashes shows that the representation derived from the FFA is able to create a distinctive semantic space between documents from different labels. Fig. 2 shows a 2D representation of four randomly-chosen classes in WoS and 20news.

8.2 Energy efficiency

Both the BNN and FFA algorithms prove to be very energy efficient. In table 9, we see that a single run of the BNN is equivalent to running the light bulb between 11 and 41 minutes, depending on the size of the dataset being processed. The FFA itself (without PCA pre-processing) has a wider range, from 7 to 81 minutes, but still remains very

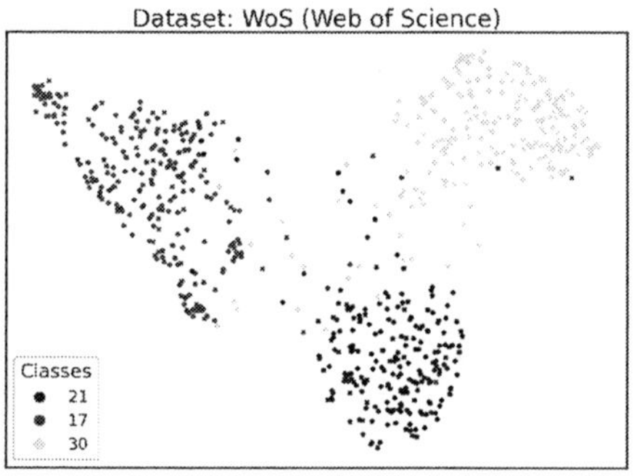

(a) neighbors=50, dist=0.1

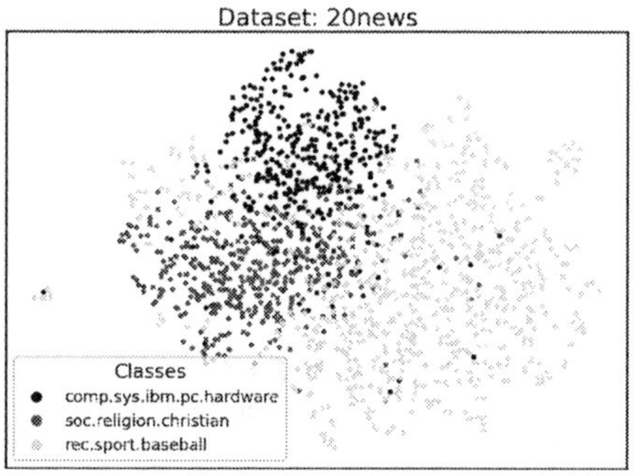

(b) neighbors=15, dist=0.8

Figure 2: Dimensionality reduction of the 128 dimension vector from FFA with UMAP. Classes are randomly selected.

[12]Library from github.com/fmfn/BayesianOptimization

affordable.

We note that the main cost of the FFA is of course evaluation. We are optimizing the algorithm on *Prec@k*, which is an expensive function to run, as it involves a computationally-intensive nearest neighbour computation. As we pointed out previously, optimizing on classification did not seem to give the best possible results for the FFA. But this aspect would require further investigation, since it is the main efficiency bottleneck for the algorithm.

We also note that when including PCA preprocessing, large datasets like agnews become more expensive to run: the highest overall consumption in the tiny models in the table comes from to the PCA on agnews (81 minutes). This is a substantial cost in getting the best out of the FFA, and one that could potentially be reduced. In particular, we are experimenting with computing dimensionality reduction on a restricted subset of our data and subsequently learning a regression function from high- to low-dimensional space to 'simulate' the effect of the PCA. Preliminary results are encouraging, with limited loss in task performance.

Lastly, the discrepancy of energy consumption is striking between our tiny models and BERT as observed in columns *BERT* and *Diff. BERT* of table 9. The latter requires a considerable larger amount of resources because of the millions of parameters being updated during fine-tuning. Across datasets, it consumes 61 times more than the average consumption of all our tiny models in a single run. Note that the difference increases according to the size of the dataset. For instance, the smallest datasets Reuters and WoS consume 7 and 12 times more than the tiny models respectively, while the largest dataset (agnews) consumes 247 times more. These results highlight the importance of putting more effort in developing smaller models because of the high energy costs of solely fine-tuning these huge models.

9 Conclusion

This paper set out to compare the respective strengths of two lightweight binary hashing algorithms, the binary neural network (BNN) and the fruit fly algorithm (FFA), on the task of generating highly-compressed document representations. We adapted the original FFA to this new context by prepending a dimensionality reduction step to the architecture, implemented with PCA. We found that the two methods display different strengths and achieved their top performance on different tasks and datasets. Both are energy-efficient, with the FFA's consumption being mostly taken by evaluation at optimization stage.

Both BNNs and biologically-inspired algorithms are relatively new in NLP, and therefore require a lot of community efforts to fully understand their respective behaviours. As immediate further work, we would perform an in-depth analysis on our datasets' distributions to understand better why some data seem more suited to one or the other algorithm, and why discrepancies emerge in the way that classification and precision at k are tackled. From an efficiency point of view, we will also further investigate how to reduce the cost of the dimensionality reduction step before applying the FFA.

One of the main strengths of both models is their low running costs. All steps can be run in a CPU or even on a mobile phone – as in the case of the BNN. This is a crucial point when it comes to providing high quality systems based on artificial intelligence models for low-resource communities. As an example application, we have integrated the PCA+FFA pipeline to the PeARS search engine.[13] PeARS implements local Internet search by allowing users to index and search Web documents on their home machine. It requires an indexing method that is as lightweight as possible for users with limited hardware resources. The FFA is a natural choice here, with its good performance on the *Prec@k* metric. We hope that the work presented in this paper will inspire other researchers to invest effort in developing lightweight techniques to solve core NLP problems, and share them with the communities that benefit from them.

Acknowledgments

We gratefully acknowledge the funding provided by the NLnet Foundation, with financial support from the European Commission's Next Generation Internet programme, under the aegis of DG Communications Networks, Content and Technology (grant agreement No 825322).

[13] `https://pearsproject.org/`, code at `https://github.com/PeARSearch/PeARS-orchard`.

References

Ashutosh Adhikari, Achyudh Ram, Raphael Tang, and Jimmy Lin. 2019a. Docbert: Bert for document classification. *arXiv preprint arXiv:1904.08398*.

Ashutosh Adhikari, Achyudh Ram, Raphael Tang, and Jimmy Lin. 2019b. Rethinking complex neural network architectures for document classification. In *Proceedings of the 2019 Conference of the North American Chapter of the Association for Computational Linguistics: Human Language Technologies, Volume 1 (Long and Short Papers)*, pages 4046–4051, Minneapolis, Minnesota. Association for Computational Linguistics.

Iz Beltagy, Matthew E Peters, and Arman Cohan. 2020. Longformer: The long-document transformer. *arXiv preprint arXiv:2004.05150*.

Emily M. Bender, Timnit Gebru, Angelina McMillan-Major, and Shmargaret Shmitchell. 2021. On the dangers of stochastic parrots: Can language models be too big? . In *Proceedings of the 2021 ACM Conference on Fairness, Accountability, and Transparency*, FAccT '21, page 610–623, New York, NY, USA. Association for Computing Machinery.

Tom Brown, Benjamin Mann, Nick Ryder, Melanie Subbiah, Jared D Kaplan, Prafulla Dhariwal, Arvind Neelakantan, Pranav Shyam, Girish Sastry, Amanda Askell, Sandhini Agarwal, Ariel Herbert-Voss, Gretchen Krueger, Tom Henighan, Rewon Child, Aditya Ramesh, Daniel Ziegler, Jeffrey Wu, Clemens Winter, Chris Hesse, Mark Chen, Eric Sigler, Mateusz Litwin, Scott Gray, Benjamin Chess, Jack Clark, Christopher Berner, Sam McCandlish, Alec Radford, Ilya Sutskever, and Dario Amodei. 2020. Language models are few-shot learners. In *Advances in Neural Information Processing Systems*, volume 33, pages 1877–1901. Curran Associates, Inc.

Suthee Chaidaroon and Yi Fang. 2017. Variational deep semantic hashing for text documents. In *Proceedings of the 40th International ACM SIGIR Conference on Research and Development in Information Retrieval*, pages 75–84.

Sanjoy Dasgupta, Charles F Stevens, and Saket Navlakha. 2017. A neural algorithm for a fundamental computing problem. *Science*, 358(6364):793–796.

Jacob Devlin, Ming-Wei Chang, Kenton Lee, and Kristina Toutanova. 2019. BERT: Pre-training of deep bidirectional transformers for language understanding. In *Proceedings of the 2019 Conference of the North American Chapter of the Association for Computational Linguistics: Human Language Technologies, Volume 1 (Long and Short Papers)*, pages 4171–4186, Minneapolis, Minnesota. Association for Computational Linguistics.

Jesse Dodge, Maarten Sap, Ana Marasović, William Agnew, Gabriel Ilharco, Dirk Groeneveld, Margaret Mitchell, and Matt Gardner. 2021. Documenting large webtext corpora: A case study on the colossal clean crawled corpus. *arXiv preprint arXiv:2104.08758*.

Casper Hansen, Christian Hansen, Jakob Grue Simonsen, Stephen Alstrup, and Christina Lioma. 2020. Unsupervised semantic hashing with pairwise reconstruction. In *Proceedings of the 43rd International ACM SIGIR Conference on Research and Development in Information Retrieval*, pages 2009–2012.

Itay Hubara, Matthieu Courbariaux, Daniel Soudry, Ran El-Yaniv, and Yoshua Bengio. 2016. Binarized neural networks. *Advances in neural information processing systems*, 29.

Kamran Kowsari, Donald E Brown, Mojtaba Heidarysafa, Kiana Jafari Meimandi, Matthew S Gerber, and Laura E Barnes. 2017. Hdltex: Hierarchical deep learning for text classification. In *2017 16th IEEE international conference on machine learning and applications (ICMLA)*, pages 364–371. IEEE.

Ken Lang. 2008. The 20 news groups data set. *http://people. csail. mit. edu/jrennie/20Newsgroups/.*

David D. Lewis. 1997. Reuters-21578 text categorization collection data set.

Yuchen Liang, Chaitanya K. Ryali, Benjamin Hoover, Leopold Grinberg, Saket Navlakha, Mohammed J. Zaki, and Dmitry Krotov. 2021. Can a fruit fly learn word embeddings?

Jingzhou Liu, Wei-Cheng Chang, Yuexin Wu, and Yiming Yang. 2017. Deep learning for extreme multi-label text classification. In *Proceedings of the 40th international ACM SIGIR conference on research and development in information retrieval*, pages 115–124.

Tomas Mikolov, Kai Chen, Greg Corrado, and Jeffrey Dean. 2013. Efficient estimation of word representations in vector space. *arXiv preprint arXiv:1301.3781*.

Nikunj Oza. 2010. Siam 2007 text mining competition dataset.

Jeffrey Pennington, Richard Socher, and Christopher D Manning. 2014. Glove: Global vectors for word representation. In *Proceedings of the 2014 conference on empirical methods in natural language processing (EMNLP)*, pages 1532–1543.

Simon Preissner and Aurélie Herbelot. 2019. To be fair: a case for cognitively-inspired models of meaning. In *Proceedings of the Sixth Italian Conference on Computational Linguistics*.

Simon Preissner and Aurélie Herbelot. 2020. Biodiversity in nlp: modelling lexical meaning with the fruit fly algorithm. *IJCoL. Italian Journal of Computational Linguistics*, 6(6-1):11–28.

Gerard Salton and J Michael. 1986. Mcgill. *Introduction to modern information retrieval*, 1(4.1):4–1.

Victor Sanh, Lysandre Debut, Julien Chaumond, and Thomas Wolf. 2019. Distilbert, a distilled version of bert: smaller, faster, cheaper and lighter. *arXiv preprint arXiv:1910.01108*.

Victor Schmidt, Kamal Goyal, Aditya Joshi, Boris Feld, Liam Conell, Nikolas Laskaris, Doug Blank, Jonathan Wilson, Sorelle Friedler, and Sasha Luccioni. 2021. CodeCarbon: Estimate and Track Carbon Emissions from Machine Learning Computing.

Emma Strubell, Ananya Ganesh, and Andrew McCallum. 2019. Energy and policy considerations for deep learning in NLP. In *Proceedings of the 57th Annual Meeting of the Association for Computational Linguistics*, pages 3645–3650, Florence, Italy. Association for Computational Linguistics.

Xiang Zhang, Junbo Zhao, and Yann LeCun. 2015. Character-level convolutional networks for text classification. *Advances in neural information processing systems*, 28.

Yifei Zhang and Hao Zhu. 2019. Doc2hash: Learning discrete latent variables for documents retrieval. In *Proceedings of the 2019 Conference of the North American Chapter of the Association for Computational Linguistics: Human Language Technologies, Volume 1 (Long and Short Papers)*, pages 2235–2240.

A Appendix

A.1 Energy consumption

dataset	LSH	BNN	PCA+Fly = FFA (Overall)	BERT
20news	0.013	0.009	0.001+0.012 = 0.14	0.365
agnews	0.022	0.028	0.058+0.054 = 0.112	13.435
reuters	0.005	0.018	0.001+0.005 = 0.006	0.192
tmc	0.012	0.011	0.003+0.011 = 0.014	0.717
wiki	0.021	0.014	0.004+0.015 = 0.018	0.854
wos	0.008	0.007	0.001+0.006 = 0.007	0.213

Table 1: Energy consumption of the models in minutes run in kWh. Figures are averages for single optimization steps. Values in red and green are the models spending the most and least energy respectively.

A.2 Model hyperparameters

SentencePiece was run with default hyperparameters and a vocabulary size of $10,000$. For the BNN, the best log-probability exponent p varied depending on the dataset: 3 for Reuters, Agnews and TMC, 4 for 20news and WoS, 5 for Wiki. For the FFA, $p = 4$ emerged as the best choice for all datasets. The number of top words t gave optimal results at $t = 300$ for most datasets, apart from WoS ($t = 500$).

Tuning the learning rate for the BNN did not result in any statistically significant changes, so all results are reported for $lr = 0.01$.

For the FFA, we tuned the projection size from 4 to 16 and the WTA rate from 10 to 70. The best hyperparameter combinations for each pair of hash size and dataset are included in the table below. The Logistic Regression classifier used the default sklearn hyperparameters, in multiclass mode.

	32 bits		64 bits		128 bits	
dataset	WTA	proj size	WTA	proj size	WTA	proj size
20news	16	70	16	50	16	50
agnews	8	50	8	30	4	50
reuters	4	50	4	50	4	50
tmc	4	50	8	50	12	30
wiki	8	50	8	30	8	30
wos	8	70	8	50	4	70

Table 2: Hyperparameters table.

Look Ma, Only 400 Samples! Revisiting the Effectiveness of Automatic N-Gram Rule Generation for Spelling Normalization in Filipino

Lorenzo Jaime Yu Flores **Dragomir Radev**
Yale University
lj.flores@yale.edu

Abstract

With 84.75 million Filipinos online, the ability for models to process online text is crucial for developing Filipino NLP applications. To this end, spelling correction is a crucial preprocessing step for downstream processing. However, the lack of data prevents the use of language models for this task. In this paper, we propose an N-Gram + Damerau-Levenshtein distance model with automatic rule extraction. We train the model on 300 samples, and show that despite limited training data, it achieves good performance and outperforms other deep learning approaches in terms of accuracy and edit distance. Moreover, the model (1) requires little compute power, (2) trains in little time, thus allowing for retraining, and (3) is easily interpretable, allowing for direct troubleshooting, highlighting the success of traditional approaches over more complex deep learning models in settings where data is unavailable.

1 Introduction

Filipinos are among the most active social media users worldwide (Baclig, 2022). In 2022, roughly 84.75M Filipinos were online (Statista, 2022a), with 96.2% on Facebook (Statista, 2022b). Hence, developing language models that can process online text is crucial for Filipino NLP applications.

Contractions and abbreviations are common in such online text (Salvacion and Limpot, 2022). For example, *dito* (here) can be written as *d2*, or *nakakatawa* (funny) as *nkktawa*, which are abbreviated based on their pronunciation. However, language models like Google Translate remain limited in their ability to detect and correct such words, as we find later in the paper. Hence, we aim to improve the spelling correction ability of such models.

In this paper, we demonstrate the effectiveness of a simple n-gram based algorithm for this task, inspired by prior work on automatic rule generation by Mangu and Brill (1997). Specifically, we (1) create a training dataset of 300 examples, (2) automatically generate n-gram based spelling rules using the dataset, and (3) use the rules to propose and select candidates. We then demonstrate that this model outperforms seq-to-seq approaches.

Ultimately, the paper aims to highlight the use of traditional approaches in areas where SOTA language models are difficult to apply due to limitations in data availability. Such approaches have the added benefit of (1) requiring little compute power for training and inference, (2) training in very little time (allowing for frequent retraining), and (3) giving researchers full clarity over its inner workings, thereby improving the ease of troubleshooting.

2 Related Work

The problem of online text spelling correction is most closely related to *spelling normalization* – the subtask of reverting shortcuts and abbreviations into their original form (Nocon et al., 2014). In this paper, we will use *correcting* to mean *normalizing* a word. This is useful for low-resource languages like Filipino, wherein spelling is often not standardized across its users (Li et al., 2020).

Many approaches have been tried for word normalization in online Filipino text: (1) *predetermined rules* using commonly seen patterns (Guingab et al., 2014; Oco and Borra, 2011), (2) *dictionary-substitution models* for extracting patterns in misspelled words (Nocon et al., 2014), or (3) *trigrams* and *Levenshtein or QWERTY distance* to select words which share similar trigrams or are close in terms of edit or keyboard distance (Chan et al., 2008; Go et al., 2017).

Each method has its limitations which we seek to address. *Predetermined rules* must be manually updated to learn emerging patterns, as is common in the constantly evolving vocabulary of online Filipino text (Salvacion and Limpot, 2022; Lumabi, 2020). *Dictionary-substitution models* are limited by the constraint of picking mapping each pattern to only a single substitution, whereas in reality, dif-

Proceedings of The Third Workshop on Simple and Efficient Natural Language Processing (SustaiNLP), pages 29 - 35
December 7, 2022 ©2022 Association for Computational Linguistics

ferent patterns may need to be applied to different words bearing the same pattern (Nocon et al., 2014). *Trigrams and distance metrics* alone may be successful in the context of correcting typographical errors for which the model was developed (Chan et al., 2008), but may not be as successful on intentionally abbreviated words. Our work uses a combination of these methods to develop a model that can be easily updated, considers multiple possible candidates, and works in the online text setting.

The task is further complicated by the lack of data, which hinders the use of large pretrained language models. Previous supervised modeling approaches require thousands of labeled examples (Etoori et al., 2018), and even unsupervised approaches for similar problems required vocabulary lists containing the desired words for translation (Lample et al., 2018a,b). Since such datasets are not available, our paper revisits simpler models, and finds that they exhibit comparable performance to that of much larger SOTA models.

3 Data

We use a dataset consisting of Facebook comments made on weather advisories of a Philippine weather bureau in 2014. We identified 403 distinct abbreviated and contracted words, and had three Filipino undergraduate volunteers write their "correct" versions. To maximize the data, we removed hyphens and standardized spacing, then filtered out candidates where all annotators gave different answers.

We obtained 398 examples (98.7%) with 83.8% inter-annotator agreement. We then created a 298-100 train-test split; we selected test examples that used spelling rules present in the training set to test the ability of our n-gram model to extract and apply such rules. To test generalizability, we also perform cross-validation. The data and code for our experiments are available at the following repository. [1]

4 Model

Automatic Rule Generation We extract spelling rules from pairs (w, c), where w is a misspelled word, and c is its corrected version. The rule generation algorithm slides a window of length k over w and c, and records $w[i:i+k] \rightarrow c[j:j+k]$ as a rule (i, j are pointers); it returns a dictionary mapping each substring to a list of "correct" substrings (See Appendix 1 for algorithm and example).

We test substrings of length 1 to 4, and find that lengths 1 / 2 work best. This makes sense as many Filipino words are abbreviated by syllable, which typically have 1-2 letters. This is similar to Indonesian (Batais and Wiltshire, 2015) and Malay (Ramli et al., 2015), suggesting possible extensions.

We further filter candidates to words present in a Filipino vocabulary list developed by Gensaya (2018) (MIT License), except for when none of the candidates exist in the vocabulary list, in which case we use all the generated words as candidates.

Candidate Generation We recursively generate candidates by replacing each substring with all possible rules in the rule dictionary. If the substring is not present, we keep the substring as is. An example can be found in Appendix D.

We find that rules involving single letter substrings often occur at the end of a word. Hence, we test candidate generation algorithms which either allow single letter rules to be used anywhere when generating (V1), or only for the last letter of a word (V2). We also vary the # of candidates kept at each generation step (ranked by likelihood, see Eq 2).

Ranking Candidates We explore two ways of ranking candidates: (1) *Damerau-Levenshtein Distance* we rank candidates based on their edit distance from the misspelled word using the pyxdameraulevenshtein[2] package with standard settings, and (2) *Likelihood Score* we compute the likelihood of the output word c given misspelled word w as the product of probability the rules used to generate it, where the probability of a rule is the number of occurrences of $a \rightarrow b$ divided by the number of rules starting with a (See Eqs 1, 2).

$$P(a \rightarrow b) = \frac{|\{a \rightarrow b\}|}{|\{a \rightarrow c\} \forall c|} \tag{1}$$

$$P(w \rightarrow c) = \prod_{i=1}^{len(w)-k} P(w[i:i+k] \rightarrow c[i:i+k]) \tag{2}$$

5 Evaluation

5.1 Comparison to Language Models

We benchmark the performance of our models against two seq-to-seq models on the same dataset: (1) **ByT5** (Xue et al., 2022): a character-level T5 model (Raffel et al., 2020) trained on cross-lingual

[1] https://github.com/ljyflores/Filipino-Slang

[2] https://github.com/lanl/pyxDamerauLevenshtein

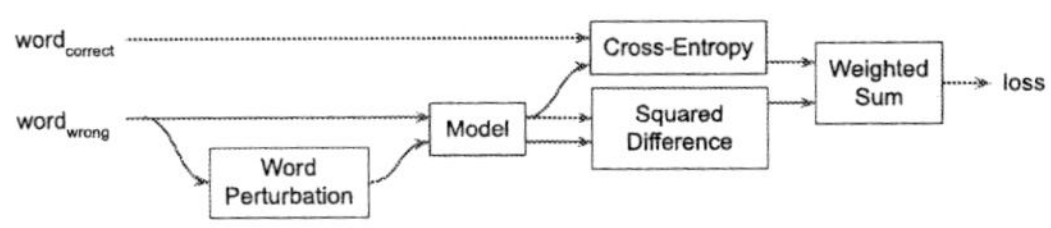

Figure 1: Π-Model Architecture (Laine and Aila, 2017)

tasks, shown to be robust to misspellings, and (2) **Roberta-Tagalog** (Cruz and Cheng, 2021): a BERT (Devlin et al., 2019) model trained on large Filipino corpora for masked language modeling. We performed hyperparameter tuning using an 80-20 split of the training data.

For inference, we obtain the top five candidates for each misspelled word by selecting the highest scoring candidates using beam search.

5.2 Augmentation Techniques

Since deep learning models perform poorly on small datasets, we use two techniques to improve performance to achieve more quality benchmarks.

First, we use Π-model (Laine and Aila, 2017) (Fig 1), a semi-supervised technique which minimizes the mean-squared distance between the predicted corrections for two versions of a misspelled word, where the weight is a hyperparameter.

Then, we use autoencoding augmentation (AE) (Bergmanis et al., 2017), where we iteratively train a seq2seq model on the original spelling normalization task and an autoencoding task, where the model is trained to reproduce the same word.

5.3 Comparison to Google Translate

We also benchmark using Google Translate's model. We input each word and check if the model outputs a valid translation or suggests a correction (i.e. "Did you mean X?"). A correct translation/correction means the model was able to correct (and thus translate) the misspelled word.

5.4 Evaluation

We evaluate the models with two metrics: (1) **Accuracy @ k:** % of observations where the target is present among the top-k candidates, and (2) **Damerau-Levenshtein Distance (DLD):** Best, average, and worst-case DLD of the top 5 candidates.

6 Results

6.1 Results from Evaluation Metrics

We train our models and show the results on the test set in Table 1 (See Appendix 3 for hyperparameter details). To test generalizability, we perform 5-fold cross-validation (See Appendix 2).

The N-Grams + DLD V1 algorithm performs best in terms of accuracy and best-case DLD. It achieves an improvement of 32% from the next best model (DLD) for accuracy @ 1, which we consider most important, as real-world spellcheckers usually suggest one word. In addition, the ByT5 + Π-Model exhibits the best average DLD; hence it generates many candidates which resemble the target, though not achieving the correct output.

Also, N-Grams + Likelihood performs much worse than with DLD, despite using the same candidate generation procedure. This was because the dictionary also had irrelevant rules which muddled the estimates; these can be filtered out with heuristics, though at the expense of generalizability.

Moreover, the Π-model results in small improvements over the original ByT5 across all metrics; this illustrates the impact of semi-supervised approaches over supervised approaches in settings with limited data, albeit with limited success.

6.2 N-Gram Algorithm Runtime

Though N-Grams + DLD V1 achieves the best performance, it performs inference in 2.781s on average. N-Grams DLD V2 achieves significantly faster performance (0.0086s) with a marginal decrease in performance (See Appendix C). It is worth noting that all N-Gram models train in under a second on a local CPU, whereas most language models required at least 20 minutes on a GPU.

6.3 Analysis of Errors: N-Gram + DLD V1

We analyze the examples in which the N-Gram + DLD did not select the correct word as the top choice (i.e. error at $k = 1$). The N-Gram + DLD model produced errors on 23 observations (out of 100); we separate these errors into those where the target was and was not in the candidate list.

Errors with Target in the Candidates There were 9 (out of 23) errors wherein the target was not among the candidates. In such cases, the DL score selected candidates which closely resembled the input, but were wrong; the correct choices were ranked in the top 12.65% of candidates on average (median of 8.57%). Given the difficulty in distinguishing between words with similar spellings, context may be required (e.g. words surrounding the misspelled words, likelihood of word occurring).

Type	Model	Accuracy @ k (%)			DLD		
		$k = 1$	$k = 3$	$k = 5$	Min	Mean	Max
N-Gram Based	N-Grams + DLD V1	**0.77**	**0.82**	**0.85**	**0.46**	2.91	4.73
	N-Grams + DLD V2	0.67	0.74	0.74	1.03	2.96	4.59
	N-Grams + Likelihood V1	0.17	0.38	0.58	1.22	3.50	5.29
	N-Grams + Likelihood V2	0.47	0.61	0.64	1.30	3.06	4.65
ByT5	Model Only	0.31	0.42	0.49	0.98	2.71	4.38
	Model + Π-Model	0.37	0.58	0.66	0.57	**2.06**	3.41
	Model + AE	0.04	0.04	0.04	4.28	6.69	10.2
Roberta-Tagalog	Model Only	0.00	0.00	0.00	5.79	15.3	56.7
	Model + Π-Model	0.00	0.00	0.00	5.69	16.5	69.2
	Model + AE	0.00	0.00	0.00	9.44	42.8	81.7
Baselines	DLD	0.45	0.67	0.72	0.59	2.28	**3.32**
	Google Translate	0.44	-	-	-	-	-

Table 1: Performance of Spelling Normalization Models on Test Set, see Appendix 3 for hyperparameter settings

Errors with Target not in the Candidates There were 14 (out of 23) errors with targets not in the candidate list; here, the rule dictionary lacked at least one rule that was necessary to correct each of the misspelled words. Upon adding these rules to the dictionary, the model correctly predicted all but five observations. In those five cases, the target was in the candidate list but not selected as the top result, suggesting the need for better ranking methods as discussed in the previous section.

As demonstrated by this section, a benefit of the N-Gram + DLD model is that it allows access to the collected rules, allowing researchers to understand the cause of such errors, and hence directly make tweaks (e.g. by adding rules, tweaking substring length k) to improve the model. In contrast, explainability remains a challenge for language models, thereby reducing their ease of troubleshooting.

7 Conclusion

In this study, we propose an N-Gram + DLD model for spelling normalization of Filipino online text, and compare it to deep learning benchmarks. The N-Gram + DLD V1 model achieves the best accuracy and best-case DLD, with a 32% improvement in accuracy @ 1 over the next best model (DLD). This shows the potential of simpler techniques, especially when data is scarce.

Besides improved performance, the N-Gram + DLD model requires little compute power and memory for training and inference. This allows for frequent retraining of the model and addition of new spelling rules as new words emerge. The model also allows researchers to understand how predictions are made, and make appropriate tweaks to the spelling rules, candidate sorting method, or hyperparameters used (e.g. length of substrings).

This work has limitations which suggest areas for improvement. First, the current work uses a small dataset limited to the weather domain. Using more diverse datasets can improve the comprehensiveness of the rule dictionary. Also, more complete dictionaries containing Filipino words and their conjugations can help filter down valid candidates before running DLD.

Second, the candidate ranking method can be improved, especially in cases where the target and selected words are similar, as discussed in the section 6.3. For example, words can be ranked by how common they are, or by inferring the correct choice from the context. This has the added benefit of reducing the candidate pool, requiring fewer DLD calculations and hence reducing inference time.

Finally, we only explore correcting misspelled words; combining it with misspelling detection can further boost the practical applications of this work.

Ultimately, the development of such models will pave the way for improvements in Filipino NLP, and enable the development of more applications that can serve the wider online Filipino community.

Acknowledgements

We would like to thank Luis Angelo Chavez, Agnes Robang, and Mirella Arguelles for annotating the dataset, and Hailey Schoelkopf and Linyong Nan for their feedback on the paper.

References

Eloisa Baclig. 2022. Social media, internet craze keep ph on top 2 of world list. *Philippine Daily Inquirer*.

Saleh Batais and Caroline Wiltshire. 2015. Word and syllable constraints in indonesian adaptation: Ot analysis. *LSA Annual Meeting Extended Abstracts*.

Toms Bergmanis, Katharina Kann, Hinrich Schütze, and Sharon Goldwater. 2017. Training data augmentation for low-resource morphological inflection. In *Proceedings of the CoNLL SIGMORPHON 2017 Shared Task: Universal Morphological Reinflection*, pages 31–39, Vancouver. Association for Computational Linguistics.

Cedric Chan, Ian Querol, Vazir Cheng, and Vazir Querol. 2008. Spellchef: Spelling checker and corrector for filipino. *Journal of Research in Science, Computing and Engineering*, 4.

Jan Christian Blaise Cruz and Charibeth Cheng. 2021. Improving large-scale language models and resources for filipino. *arXiv preprint arXiv:2111.06053*.

Jacob Devlin, Ming-Wei Chang, Kenton Lee, and Kristina Toutanova. 2019. BERT: Pre-training of deep bidirectional transformers for language understanding. In *Proceedings of the 2019 Conference of the North American Chapter of the Association for Computational Linguistics: Human Language Technologies, Volume 1 (Long and Short Papers)*, pages 4171–4186, Minneapolis, Minnesota. Association for Computational Linguistics.

Pravallika Etoori, Manoj Chinnakotla, and Radhika Mamidi. 2018. Automatic spelling correction for resource-scarce languages using deep learning. In *Proceedings of ACL 2018, Student Research Workshop*, pages 146–152, Melbourne, Australia. Association for Computational Linguistics.

Carl Jerwin F. Gensaya. 2018. Tagalog words stemmer using python. `https://github.com/crlwingen/TagalogStemmerPython`.

Matthew Phillip Go, Nicco Nocon, and Allan Borra. 2017. Gramatika: A grammar checker for the low-resourced filipino language. In *TENCON 2017 - 2017 IEEE Region 10 Conference*, pages 471–475.

Ceflyn Guingab, Karen Alexandra Palma, Jerome Layron, Ria Sagum, and Ferdonico Tamayo. 2014. Filitenor: Text normalization tool for filipino. In *Proceedings of the 10th National Natural Language Processing Research Symposium*.

Samuli Laine and Timo Aila. 2017. Temporal ensembling for semi-supervised learning. In *5th International Conference on Learning Representations, ICLR 2017, Toulon, France, April 24-26, 2017, Conference Track Proceedings*. OpenReview.net.

Guillaume Lample, Alexis Conneau, Marc'Aurelio Ranzato, Ludovic Denoyer, and Hervé Jégou. 2018a. Word translation without parallel data. In *6th International Conference on Learning Representations, ICLR 2018, Vancouver, BC, Canada, April 30 - May 3, 2018, Conference Track Proceedings*.

Guillaume Lample, Myle Ott, Alexis Conneau, Ludovic Denoyer, and Marc'Aurelio Ranzato. 2018b. Phrase-based & neural unsupervised machine translation. In *Proceedings of the 2018 Conference on Empirical Methods in Natural Language Processing*, pages 5039–5049, Brussels, Belgium. Association for Computational Linguistics.

Yiyuan Li, Antonios Anastasopoulos, and Alan W Black. 2020. Comparison of interactive knowledge base spelling correction models for low-resource languages. arXiv.

Bethany Marie Lumabi. 2020. The lexical trend of backward speech among filipino millenials on facebook. *International Journal of English and Comparative Literary Studies*, 1:44–54.

Lidia Mangu and Eric Brill. 1997. Automatic rule acquisition for spelling correction. In *Proceedings of the Fourteenth International Conference on Machine Learning*, ICML '97, page 187–194, San Francisco, CA, USA. Morgan Kaufmann Publishers Inc.

Nicco Nocon, Gems Cuevas, Jedd Gopez, and Peter Suministrado. 2014. Norm: A text normalization system for filipino shortcut texts using the dictionary substitution approach. In *Proceedings of the 10th National Natural Language Processing Research Symposium*.

Nathaniel Oco and Allan Borra. 2011. A grammar checker for Tagalog using LanguageTool. In *Proceedings of the 9th Workshop on Asian Language Resources*, pages 2–9, Chiang Mai, Thailand. Asian Federation of Natural Language Processing.

Colin Raffel, Noam Shazeer, Adam Roberts, Katherine Lee, Sharan Narang, Michael Matena, Yanqi Zhou, Wei Li, and Peter J. Liu. 2020. Exploring the limits of transfer learning with a unified text-to-text transformer. *J. Mach. Learn. Res.*, 21(1).

Izzad Ramli, Nursuriati Jamil, Noraini Seman, and Norizah Ardi. 2015. An improved syllabification for a better malay language text-to-speech synthesis (tts). *Procedia Computer Science*, 76:417–424.

Justine Daphnie Salvacion and Marilou Y. Limpot. 2022. Linguistic features of filipino netspeak in online conversations. *International Journal of Multidisciplinary Research*, 8:171–177.

Statista. 2022a. Number of internet users in the philippines from 2017 to 2020, with forecasts until 2026.

Statista. 2022b. Number of internet users in the philippines from 2017 to 2020, with forecasts until 2026.

Linting Xue, Aditya Barua, Noah Constant, Rami Al-Rfou, Sharan Narang, Mihir Kale, Adam Roberts, and Colin Raffel. 2022. ByT5: Towards a token-free future with pre-trained byte-to-byte models. *Transactions of the Association for Computational Linguistics*, 10:291–306.

A Cross Validation Results

The cross validated results are shown in Table 2. While the metrics dropped from that in Table 1, the models still exhibit the same order of performance in terms of accuracy.

B Algorithms

Algorithm 1 Automatic Rule Generation

Input w (wrong word), r (right word)
Output d (rule dictionary)

$k, d \leftarrow \{\}, ptr_w = 0, ptr_r = 0$
while $ptr_w < len(w)$ & $ptr_r < len(r)$ **do**
  $substr_w \leftarrow w[ptr_w : ptr_w + k]$
  $substr_r \leftarrow r[ptr_r : ptr_r + k]$
  if $substr_w = substr_r$ **then**
    $ptr_w \leftarrow ptr_w + k$
    $ptr_r \leftarrow ptr_r + k$
  else
    $ptr_w \leftarrow ptr_w + 1$
    $ptr_r \leftarrow ptr_r + k$
  end if
  Append $substr_r$ to key $substr_w$ in d
end while
Return d

```
{'21': ['tu', 'ka', 'tu', '21', 'tu'],
 'lo': ['lo', 'lu', 'lo', 'lo'],
 'y':  ['y'],
 'ul': ['ul'],
 'lu': ['lu'],
 'uy': ['uy'],
 'n':  ['n', 'in', 'n', 'ya', 'na', 'ng',...]
```

Figure 2: Example of a generated rule dictionary

C Runtime Performance

We plot accuracy @ 1 and runtime in Figures 3 and 4 respectively, and find that using a cutoff of 100 and 30 for N-Grams + DLD and N-Grams + Likelihood respectively achieve the best tradeoff between runtime and performance.

D Example

Figure 5 shows a rule dictionary and how the rules are used to normalize *"2loy"* to *"tuloy"*.

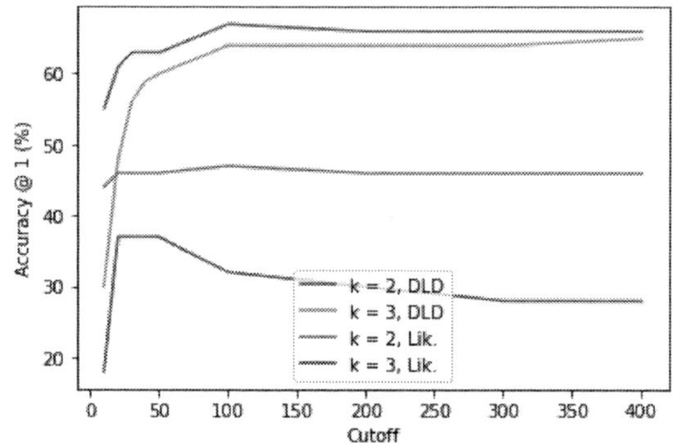

Figure 3: N-Gram Cutoff vs. Test Set Accuracy @ 1 (%), k is the maximum length of substring considered

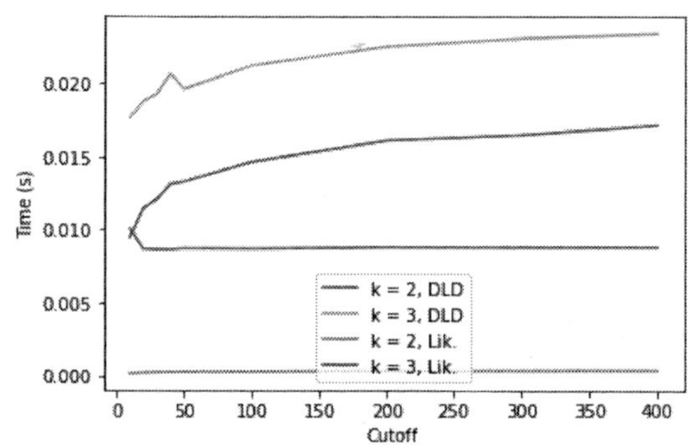

Figure 4: N-Gram Cutoff vs. Inference Time (s), k is the maximum length of substring considered

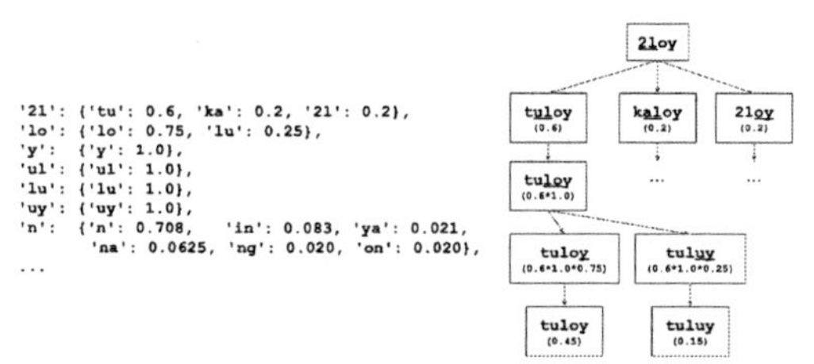

Figure 5: Example Inference for *"2loy"*

E Computational Details

We use one RTX 3090 (24GiB) GPU to perform training for the language models, and we used a total of six GPU hours across finetuning and hyperparameter selection. We note that ByT5 consists of 300 million parameters.

F Hyperparameter Settings

We train all models with the Adam optimizer, with a starting learning rate of 5e−5 and stability of

Model	Accuracy @ k (%)			DLD		
	$k=1$	$k=3$	$k=5$	Min	Mean	Max
RT	0.0 ± 0.00	0.0 ± 0.00	0.0 ± 0.00	6.06 ± 0.55	12.0 ± 2.85	46.2 ± 20.0
RT + Π	0.0 ± 0.00	0.0 ± 0.00	0.0 ± 0.00	6.08 ± 0.56	15.3 ± 2.77	61.7 ± 17.5
RT + AE	0.0 ± 0.00	0.00 ± 0.00	0.00 ± 0.00	7.38 ± 1.53	21.3 ± 6.92	54.9 ± 8.10
BT	0.32 ± 0.06	0.52 ± 0.05	0.59 ± 0.07	0.77 ± 0.15	2.31 ± 0.16	3.76 ± 0.26
BT + Π	0.40 ± 0.06	0.57 ± 0.03	0.65 ± 0.03	0.53 ± 0.05	1.75 ± 0.07	2.83 ± 0.12
BT + AE	0.02 ± 0.03	0.02 ± 0.03	0.02 ± 0.03	4.05 ± 0.41	6.33 ± 0.38	9.45 ± 0.71
NG + DLD	0.53 ± 0.02	0.63 ± 0.04	0.65 ± 0.06	1.49 ± 0.11	2.93 ± 0.07	4.18 ± 0.11
NG + Lik.	0.35 ± 0.07	0.47 ± 0.08	0.49 ± 0.07	1.69 ± 0.26	2.95 ± 0.11	4.13 ± 0.16

Table 2: Five-fold cross validation results for models on joint train and test set, within one standard deviation Legend: RT (Roberta-Tagalog), BT (ByT5), NG (N-Grams)

1e−8. Hyperparameters were finetuned using Ray Tune, and models were selected based on the lowest validation loss, as shown in Table 3.

Model	Batch	Epochs	MSE Weight
RT	8	10	-
RT + Π	8	30	0.2
RT + AE	4	70	-
BT	1	50	-
BT + Π	1	70	0.2
BT + AE	4	70	-

Table 3: Hyperparameter settings for best models, finetuned using the Ray Tune Python library; We tried 10, 30, 50, 70 epochs, and batch sizes of 1, 2, 4, 8, and 16; Legend: RT (Roberta-Tagalog), BT (ByT5), NG (N-Grams)

Who Says Elephants Can't Run: Bringing Large Scale MoE Models into Cloud Scale Production

Young Jin Kim
Microsoft
youki@microsoft.com

Rawn Henry
NVIDIA
rhenry@nvidia.com

Raffy Fahim
Microsoft
raffybekheit@microsoft.com

Hany Hassan Awadalla
Microsoft
hanyh@microsoft.com

Abstract

Mixture of Experts (MoE) models with conditional execution of sparsely activated layers have enabled training models with a much larger number of parameters. As a result, these models have achieved significantly better quality on various natural language processing tasks including machine translation. However, it remains challenging to deploy such models in real-life scenarios due to the large memory requirements and inefficient inference. In this work, we introduce a highly efficient inference framework with several optimization approaches to accelerate the computation of sparse models and cut down the memory consumption significantly. While we achieve up to 26x speed-up in terms of throughput, we also reduce the model size almost to one eighth of the original 32-bit float model by quantizing expert weights into 4-bit integers. As a result, we are able to deploy 136x larger models with 27% less cost and significantly better quality compared to the existing solutions. This enables a paradigm shift in deploying large scale multilingual MoE transformers models replacing the traditional practice of distilling teacher models into dozens of smaller models per language or task.

1 Introduction

Transformer models are getting larger and better on a continuous basis. The largest transformer models scale up to hundreds of billions of parameters, (Smith et al., 2022) resulting in high training and inference costs. This makes it difficult to deploy such models in any real-life scenario with reasonable latency and throughput. Mixture of Experts (MoE) models offer a more cost-effective method to scaling model sizes by using sparsely activated computations. More specifically, feed forward layers can be easily enlarged by replicating the original weights E times where E is the number of experts. Each of these replicas is referred to as an expert, and tokens get routed to these experts depending on a gating function. Transformer models have a much larger number of parameters when utilizing these MoE layers. However, the number of flops remains comparable to their dense counterparts thanks to sub-linear scaling in computation costs (Shazeer et al., 2017). Recently, the Mixture of Experts (MoE) architecture has been successfully utilized to scale massive large scale multilingual models (Lepikhin et al., 2020)), NLU tasks (Fedus et al., 2021; Zoph et al., 2022) and multilingual multitask models (Kim et al., 2021).

MoE offers the benefits of scaling the model to gain better accuracy without paying the huge compute cost of massive dense models. However, large scale MoE models bring their own set of unique challenges to get efficient training and inference methods. Most of the previous work focused on improving training efficiency and throughput (Fedus et al., 2021; Kim et al., 2021). In this work, we focus on optimizing MoE models inference and latency since it is crucial to harvest the benefits of such models in real-life scenarios.

Production-scale Multilingual Machine Translation systems: in this work, we explore deploying MoE models for large scale Multilingual Machine Translation systems to benefit from large language models, while maintaining reasonable serving cost. Multilingual large scale systems are already very attractive due to multiple aspects. First, they benefit modeling since they allow better accuracy, especially through transfer learning across languages. Additionally, they improve deployment and serving since we can replace dozens of models with a single model that is able to serve many languages at the same time. Nevertheless, we need the infer-

Proceedings of The Third Workshop on Simple and Efficient Natural Language Processing (SustaiNLP), pages 36 - 43
December 7, 2022

ence to be highly optimized to make inference cost-efficient. Despite these benefits, shipping such multilingual models brings a new challenge, because they usually require a much larger model capacity in terms of the number of parameters and the computation. The MoE model architecture could be a promising solution given its sub-linear or constant FLOPs increase in terms of the number of model parameters. But, the large memory consumption issue still remains.

In this work, we show how to enable deploying a single MoE model that can serve many languages replacing dozens of traditional models while improving accuracy and maintaining latency, throughput and cost efficiency. We set the goal for this work to match latency and throughput of a distilled small model deployed on CPU while achieving better serving cost.

It is worth noting that while the optimizations presented here are applied to MoE encoder-decoder architecture for multilingual machine translation task, they are applicable to other architectures and tasks without any loss of generality. Given the recent success of MoE models on wide set of NLU and NLG tasks (Fedus et al., 2021; Zoph et al., 2022), we believe the optimization presented in this work will be equally enabling to other tasks as it is for machine translation.

2 Challenges and Contributions

2.1 MoE Inference challenge

Even though the MoE architecture in theory requires much less computation with larger number of parameters, it adds several computations such as token routing and all-to-all communication which could be a significant hit to the training throughput as much as 12% for a single node as shown in (Liu et al., 2022). In addition, it significantly increases the amount of memory traffic in the MoE layers. So far, previous studies focused more on the training efficiency of those MoE models and there has not been a solution to deploy this kind of models into the real-time applications. At inference time, we have observed the naive implementation of MoE models could be up to 30 times slower than its dense counterpart with the same embedding and hidden dimensions. To achieve a reasonable deployment cost, it is critical to lower the inference cost by increasing throughput and reducing the latency. Since MoE layers are not widely optimized for the inference scenarios, it is challenging to build efficient runtime environment in terms of computation and memory consumption.

Recently, (Rajbhandari et al., 2022) introduced several approaches to improve inference of MoE models focusing on very large scale models larger than 100B parameters and decoding on multiple GPUs. When the model size increases beyond the memory limit of a single GPU, multiple GPUs can be used together for a single inference by splitting the model weights across different GPUs. While multi-gpu can reduce latency and is required to serve extremely large models, it introduces significant communication overhead and makes it more difficult to scale up and down the number of instances based on traffic. Therefore, even though multiple GPUs could bring much larger models into production, we focus on the single GPU inference scenario due to its cost efficiency with reasonably sized models. It is worth noting that the optimization we are presenting here for single GPU can be utilized for larger models on several GPUs as well. However, this is beyond the scope of this paper.

2.2 Inference Optimization Contributions

In this paper, we show how to reduce the memory requirements to deploy largest possible model on a single GPU, which avoids costly all-to-all collectives. In addition, we optimized routing efficiency for GPUs and implemented batch pruning. We describe how we extend NVIDIA's FasterTransformer[1] inference framework to support the MoE model architecture in a real world deployment scenario:

- We present how we utilize the parallel primitives in the CUTLASS[2] and CUB [3] libraries to efficiently express token routing and the batched matrix multiply required for MoE.

- We propose a new GEMM (GEneral Matrix Multiply) which can consume 4-bit/8-bit quantized weights and perform float math. The new GEMM works as drop-in replacements of normal feedforward layers without having additional logic to handle quantization/dequantization of activations. We also show that 4/8 bit weight-only quantization preserves the accuracy without any additional algorithms.

[1]https://github.com/NVIDIA/FasterTransformer
[2]https://github.com/NVIDIA/cutlass
[3]https://github.com/NVIDIA/cub

- We implement an effective batch pruning algorithm for MoE layers to make the search algorithm on the decoder very efficient.

2.3 FasterTransformer overview

We build our MoE optimization over NVIDIA's FasterTransfomer, a highly optimized open source inference engine for transformer models. FasterTransformer implements a highly optimized transformer layers for both the encoder and decoder for inference which is built on top of CUDA, cuBLAS, cuBLASLt and C++. FasterTransformer supports seamless integration with Triton Inference server [4] which enabled us to deploy our models in scalable large scale cloud environment.

We have extended FasterTransformer to support DeepSpeed MoE models(Kim et al., 2021) and added support for Transformer with Untied Positional Encoding (TUPE) (Ke et al., 2020) attention, gate routing and efficient computation of MoE layers, including batch pruning in those layers.

3 MoE Inference Optimizations

3.1 Model architecture

MoE showed tremendous success with encoder-decoder model architecture in Multilingual Machine Translation (Lepikhin et al., 2020; Kim et al., 2021), and in Natural Language understanding (Fedus et al., 2021; Zoph et al., 2022). Therefore, in this work we focus on the encoder-decoder architecture without loss of generality since the optimization is directly applicable to encoder-only and decoder-only models as well.

We train an encoder-decoder model for machine translation with deep encoder and shallow decoder architecture as proposed in (Kim et al., 2019; Kasai et al., 2020). For a given batch of input sentences, the encoder is executed only once while the decoder is executed multiple times with a beam search algorithm per token. The auto-regressive execution of the decoder is usually the performance bottleneck. Therefore, utilizing a shallow decoder partially mitigates that effect. Empirically, we have found that using half number of decoder layers than the number of encoder layers gives a good trade-off between quality and performance. For the most efficient MoE layer execution, we use top-1 gating algorithm proposed in Switch transformers (Fedus et al., 2021). At every other layer, MoE layer is used instead of the plain feedforward layer.

[4]https://github.com/triton-inference-server/server

We use embedding dimension of 1024, the positional and word correlations are computed separately and added together in the self attention module (TUPE) (Ke et al., 2020). The feed-forward hidden dimension is 4096 with 24 encoder layers and 12 decoder layers as proposed in (Kim et al., 2021). This model configuration satisfies the deep encoder and shallow decoder design and the model weights fit well into the GPU memory without tensor slicing model parallelism (Shazeer et al., 2018). The tensor slicing approach increases communication overheads and could potentially introduce training instability issues. In the production setting, we choose a model building pipeline which could minimize such instability. On the other hand, expert parallelism is preferred over tensor slicing model parallelism because an atomic layer operation such as a feedforward layer is executed inside one GPU. Therefore, we increase the number of model parameters by adding more experts. With the size of the layers and the number of layers, the total number of parameters is roughly 5 billion when 32 experts are used in the MoE layers. With half precision floating point (fp16), this is about 10 GB which can fit on a single 16 GB GPU.

3.2 Multilingual Machine Translation Model

The traditional Machine Translation deployment paradigm generally follows the teacher-student model. Where several teachers are being distilled into a very small student model that get deployed on CPU (Kim et al., 2019). For instance, deploying 100 languages translation system, would require training, distilling and deploying at least 200 of such models. Each model is trained individually for a particular language pair. This is not scalable since each individual model needs to go through various model compression steps to be deployed on CPUs with relatively low FLOPs numbers. This not only hinders scalable model building, but also knowledge sharing and transfer between different language pairs and tasks. Multilingual training approaches have been utilized to overcome this problem. However, shipping these multilingual models brings a new challenge since such models usually require much larger capacity in terms of the number of parameters and the computation.

In this work, we use a multilingual MT system trained on 10 language pairs and can be used in place of individual systems per language pair. The model is trained using production scale training

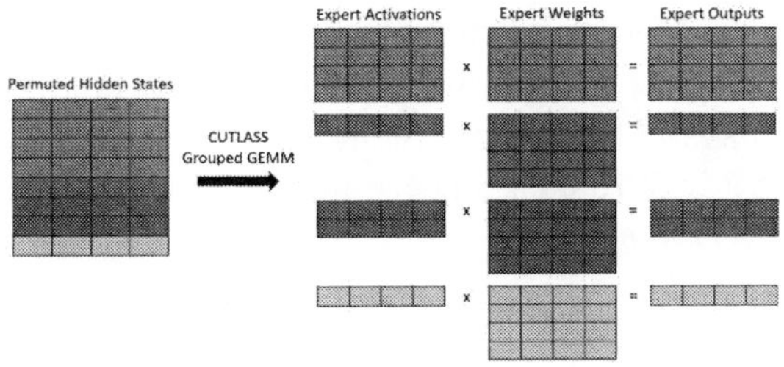

Figure 1: Shows the computation performed by CUTLASS Grouped GEMM. Each color is a sub-matrix for a particular expert, with the matrix multiplies for each expert happening in parallel. If the yellow sentence was finished, it would be omitted from the computation with batch-pruning enabled. This would completely remove the need to load the weight matrix for the yellow expert.

data of up to $\sim$ 4B training sentence pairs with a vocabulary of 128K using Sentence Piece [5]

3.3 Optimized GPU kernel design

One key factor to get an optimal performance with massive CUDA cores is to have efficient parallel algorithms for various additional operations for MoE. In MoE layers, each row in the input activation must get routed to a specific expert weight matrix, depending on a top-k gating function. We implement this routing as a GPU friendly radix sort using NVIDIA's highly efficient CUB library.

In this case, each row in the activation matrix is a token to be translated. The top-k gating function outputs a list with k $(expert\_scale, expert\_idx)$ tuples for each input token. Thus, for top-1 gating (as is done in our case), the function outputs a single tuple for every row of the activation matrix.

In order to perform the routing, we first append the index for each row to the end of the tuple giving a tuple of $(expert\_scale, expert\_idx, row\_idx)$. Then, we sort the tuple using $expert\_idx$ as the keys in order to group all rows that will be processed by the same $expert\_idx$ together. The row_idx entry from the sorted tuples are then used to permute the original activation matrix in global memory to a layout where all rows routed to the same expert are laid out contiguously in memory.

In order to finalize the routing, we view each group of rows assigned to a particular expert as its own sub-matrix and compute pointers to the start of these sub-matrices. We then pair each sub-matrix pointer with pointers to the weights and biases for the expert they are routed to, and use CUTLASS Grouped GEMM to compute all of these matrix multiplies in parallel using a single kernel. Figure 1 shows the computation performed by CUTLASS.

Finally, we un-permute the rows to their original ordering and apply the expert_scale to each row before passing the output of the MoE module to the other parts of the network.

[5] https://github.com/google/sentencepiece

3.4 Expert quantization with 4-bit and 8-bit

We quantize the MoE weights for two reasons:

1. MoE weights are extremely large which limits the size of the models that can fit on the common 16 GB inference cards such as T4.

2. MoE matrix multiplies require loading the weights for several different experts which results in them being memory bound.

We do not use Quantization Aware Training (QAT) (Wu et al., 2020), because our quantization approach does not degrade model performance. QAT is usually used when there exists a noticeable performance degradation from quantization. Also, we focus on quantizing expert weights only, because they are contributing to more than 90% of entire model weights thanks to the special property of MoE model size scaling. We get much larger model mostly from the expert parameters in MoE layers (Shazeer et al., 2017).

Algorithm 1: Weight dequantize

Input : E - Number of Experts
Input : W - quantized weights of shape (E, M, N)
Input : S - FP16 scales of shape $(E, 1, N)$
Output : FP16 dequantized weights

```
W_dq ← NewMatrix(E, M, N)
for e ← 0 to E − 1 do
    for m ← 0 to M − 1 do
        for n ← 0 to N − 1 do
            f = IntToFloat(W[e, m, n])
            W_dq[e, m, n] = f * S[e, n]
        end for
    end for
end for
return W_dq
```

All activations and biases are kept as FP16 and only the expert weight matrices are quantized. As a result, we do not require any post-training calibration (because we don't need scales for the activations) which makes this recipe easy to apply to several language families. We perform symmetric, range-based per-channel quantization on each expert weight. This means that for expert weights of shape (E, M, N) where E is the number of experts and M and N are arbitrary dimensions, we produce scales of shape $(E, 1, N)$. The same quantization method is used for int4 and int8. During inference, we dequantize the weights to FP16 and perform our matrix multiplies using floating point computations. Algorithm 1 shows the dequantization performed during inference.

One option for implementing the GEMM + Dequantize would be to write a separate kernel to dequantize the weights before the MoE GEMM. However, this would actually increase the amount of memory traffic as we would add a read of W and a write to W_{dq} as shown in Algorithm 1. As a result, we decided to take advantage of the flexibility of CUTLASS and fuse the dequantize step into the GEMM kernel. After profiling, we realized that the conversion from int to float (line 5 in Algorithm 1) was slower than anticipated. In order to improve this, we replaced the native int to float conversion (I2F) with a series of high throughput ALU and FP16 instructions which improved the performance of our fused GEMM + Dequantize.

3.4.1 Quantization Optimization

The conversion optimization mentioned above produces exact results to the native I2F conversions. It relies on two key observations.

1. For any FP16 number X where $1024 \leq X < 2048$, 1024 will be represented exactly in the exponent bits and $int(X - 1024)$ will be directly stored in the mantissa. For example, FP16 representation of 1027 (represented as 0x6403) has the integer 3 stored directly in the mantissa bits of its representation.

2. For any integer $0 \leq Y < 1024$, we can construct the FP16 representation of $Y + 1024$ by setting the exponent to 1024 and storing Y in the FP16 mantissa. This is easily done by performing 0x6400 | Y, since 0x6400 is the hex representation of 1024 in FP16.

Our optimization exploits these observations to quickly convert int4s or int8s and FP16. After we quantize the weights, we add 128 to int8 weights and 8 to int4 weights to make them all unsigned. We refer to these weights as W_+. This is not strictly necessary, but removes the need to perform sign extension logic.

3.4.2 Optimized 8-bit Dequantize

In order to best utilize the hardware, we convert int8s to FP16s two at a time, leveraging the fact that 2 FP16 elements can fit in a 32-bit register. This is done as follows:

1. We load 4 int8 values, $[e_0, e_1, e_2, e_3]$ from W_+ into a single 32-bit register.

2. We then create a second 32-bit register, R_1, that stores the FP16 representation of $[e_0 + 1024, e_1 + 1024]$ leveraging observation (2).

3. Next, we use float math to subtract $[1152, 1152]$ from R_1. This subtraction is due to the fact that we must subtract 1024 from each number in R_1 convert e_0 and e_1 to FP16. Then, we must further subtract 128 from each number to obtain the float representation of the original, signed integer.

4. Lastly, we repeat steps 2 and 3 for e_2 and e_3.

3.4.3 Optimized 4-bit Dequantize

We change the layout of the weights to reduce the number of logic instructions needed to construct the FP16s $[e_i + 1024, e_{i+1} + 1024]$. Thus, for int4, we change the layout of W_+ to reorder groups of 8 elements as follows:

$$[e_0, e_1, e_2, e_3, e_4, e_5, e_6, e_7] \rightarrow [e_0, e_2, e_4, e_6, e_1, e_3, e_5, e_7]$$

With this new layout, the idea for int4 is similar to what was previously described for int8. Of course, we must now subtract $[1032, 1032]$ to recover the original, signed integer as fp16. We must also iterate 4 times since 1 32-bit register holds 8 int4s and conversion happens 2 at a time.

3.5 MoE Batch Pruning

Batch pruning refers to the act of removing sentences from a batch dynamically as soon as they are done translating. We observed that this speeds up MoE layers as it can prevent the loading of entire expert weights, reducing the amount of memory traffic required in these memory bound layers.

In order to implement batch pruning in the MoE layers, we make a simple modification to the gating function so that it assigns a large expert_idx to all finished sentences. This causes all finished sentences to be moved to the end of the permuted activation matrix in the routing step. To complete

Table 1: Throughput of quanitzed MoE GEMMs normalized against the throughput of the FP16 MoE Gemm. The number of active experts is the number of experts that receive tokens from routing. The matrix shapes for the GEMM C = A @ B are A=mx1024, B=1024x4096, where m is different for each expert. The total number of tokens is set to 40 since this is close to what the decoder computes in our inference environment.

Active Experts	FP16	Int8 native I2F	Int8 optimized I2F	Int4 optimized I2F
1	1	1.05	1.28	1.24
4	1	1.01	1.21	1.28
8	1	1.34	1.21	1.57
16	1	1.40	1.39	1.73
24	1	1.40	1.49	1.78
32	1	1.46	1.59	1.85
GEOMEAN	1	1.26	1.35	1.56

the pruning, we simply keep track of the total number of active tokens and only process the first active_tokens rows of the permuted activation matrix mentioned in section 3.3.

4 Results and discussion

All experiments in this section are run on a single NVIDIA PCIE V100 running inside a docker container running Ubuntu 20.04 and CUDA 11.6. All code is compiled with nvcc and gcc/g++ 9.3.

We run our experiments considering an encoder-decoder MoE model with 32 experts with TUPE (Ke et al., 2020), similar to the setup in (Kim et al., 2021) but with a vocabulary size of 128k. All throughput metrics measure the time to translate 1000 tokenized English sentences ($\sim$ 40K tokens) to German (en-de) or vice-versa (de-en) and record the total number of input tokens translated per second. BLEU metrics are reported on the same data set.

4.1 Speed-up and Cost-Effectiveness

We measure the improvement of our batch pruning optimization by comparing the throughput with and without that optimization. We found that we achieve up to 1.14$\times$ speed up relative to our optimized baseline without batch pruning.

INT8/INT4 GEMM Performance. First, Table 1 shows a performance comparison for the FP16 GEMM compared to fused GEMM + Dequantize with native I2F and our optimized I2F sequence for INT8. Our INT4 implementation only supports the optimized I2F sequence. Depending on the number of experts, INT8 and INT4 could accelerate MoE computation up to 59% and 85%, respectively.

INT8/INT4 Quality Impact. We also consider the impact of INT8 and INT4 expert quantization on BLEU scores, we observe negligible translation quality degradation when quantizing model weights. Table 2 shows the change in BLEU compared to FP16 after applying quantization.

End-to-end Performance Improvements. Table 3 shows our machine translation experiments for EN-DE, with different batch sizes and different quantization schemes and reports both the throughput of our PyTorch and Faster Transformer implementations. Compared to the Torch-FP16 baselines, the optimizations applied achieve significant speed-up across different settings.

Cost Comparison. Table 4 shows the deployment cost comparison between the MoE models and smaller models optimized for CPU deployment (Kim et al., 2019). The cost of deploying MoE models which are 136x larger on CPU is more than 100 times of the cost of deploying smaller models on CPU. However, the optimized large MoE models on GPU cost less than the current CPU model deployment with smaller models.

Table 2: BLEU differences from INT8 and INT4 weight-only compared to the FP16 baseline.

Language Pair	Beam 1 Δ BLEU	
	INT8	INT4
EN-DE (Beam 1)	-0.028	-0.052
EN-DE (Beam 2)	0.051	-0.180
DE-EN (Beam 1)	-0.084	0.044
DE-EN (Beam 2)	-0.027	-0.031
Avg. of 10 language pairs (Beam 2)	-0.007	-0.167

5 Conclusions and Future Work

This paper describes how to make large MoE models cost-efficient on a single GPU in a real-world inference environment. The final implementation achieves a speedup of up to 26X over PyTorch baseline. Our GPU MoE implementation allows serving much larger and higher-quality models compared to dense models on CPUs without increasing the cost of serving. We consider two main avenues for future work. We are currently working on improving our fused GEMM + Dequantize kernel to enable the use of fully vectorized 16 byte loads on the weight matrix. In addition, we plan to explore deploying even larger models with distributed inference in the future in a cost-efficient way.

Table 3: Throughputs for beam=1 and beam=2 for varying batch sizes. Throughput is measured as input tokens processed per second. The precisions (FT-INT8 and FT-INT4) in the table refer to the quantization applied to the MoE weights. *Torch-FP16* columns show the throughput numbers when we run the model with PyTorch v1.10 using FP16 model weights.

Batch Size	Beam=1 Input tokens processed/sec				Beam=2 Input tokens processed/sec			
	Torch-FP16	FT-FP16	FT-INT8	FT-INT4	Torch-FP16	FT-FP16	FT-INT8	FT-INT4
1	16	388	401	400	14	351	361	361
8	70	1594	1639	1662	65	1453	1507	1518
20	150	3025	3178	3247	139	2571	2719	2803
32	214	4008	4264	4379	202	2960	3137	3239
64	379	5371	5706	5935	349	4333	4578	4746
96	485	6689	7101	7483	440	5062	5384	5605

Table 4: Deployment cost comparison. We show the most cost-effective throughputs under our 1s latency budget.

Hardware	Parameters	Batch size	Price (East US)	Latency (ms)	Throughput (words/sec)	Monthly USD/token
CPU (AVX512)	0.04 B	1	\$587.65 (F16s)	75	351	0.209
CPU (AVX512)	5.32 B	1	\$587.65 (F16s)	1080	26	22.602
NVIDIA T4	5.32 B	20	\$390.55 (NC4as T4 v3)	421	1565	0.250
NVIDIA T4	5.32 B	64	\$390.55 (NC4as T4 v3)	824	2560	0.153

Ethics Statement

The authors have put the best effort to comply with the ACL Ethics Policy. For the experiments, we have used WMT public domain datasets and respected the license policy for our usage.

Acknowledgements

We thank the Microsoft Z-Code team and the Microsoft Translator team for the great effort to push the limit of the production quality in machine translation and to quickly adopt the state-of-the-art Mixture of Experts models into the cloud-scale production. We also thank the Microsoft DeepSpeed team for the collaboration on more efficient and scalable Mixture of Experts architecture and library development. Additionally, we are deeply grateful for the amazing work of the NVIDIA CUTLASS team which developed grouped GEMM kernels which were crucial to get good performance with Mixture of Experts. We also thank the CUTLASS team for answering all of our questions to help us implement efficient kernels that handle GEMMs with different input types. Lastly, we thank the NVIDIA FasterTransformer team for their help with integrating our Mixture of Experts implementation into their efficient transformer inference framework.

References

William Fedus, Barret Zoph, and Noam Shazeer. 2021. Switch transformers: Scaling to trillion parameter models with simple and efficient sparsity.

Jungo Kasai, Nikolaos Pappas, Hao Peng, James Cross, and Noah A Smith. 2020. Deep encoder, shallow decoder: Reevaluating non-autoregressive machine translation. *arXiv preprint arXiv:2006.10369*.

Guolin Ke, Di He, and Tie-Yan Liu. 2020. Rethinking positional encoding in language pre-training. *CoRR*, abs/2006.15595.

Young Jin Kim, Ammar Ahmad Awan, Alexandre Muzio, Andres Felipe Cruz Salinas, Liyang Lu, Amr Hendy, Samyam Rajbhandari, Yuxiong He, and Hany Hassan Awadalla. 2021. Scalable and efficient moe training for multitask multilingual models. *arXiv preprint arXiv:2109.10465*.

Young Jin Kim, Marcin Junczys-Dowmunt, Hany Hassan, Alham Fikri Aji, Kenneth Heafield, Roman Grundkiewicz, and Nikolay Bogoychev. 2019. From research to production and back: Ludicrously fast neural machine translation. In *Proceedings of the 3rd Workshop on Neural Generation and Translation*, pages 280–288.

Dmitry Lepikhin, HyoukJoong Lee, Yuanzhong Xu, Dehao Chen, Orhan Firat, Yanping Huang, Maxim Krikun, Noam Shazeer, and Zhifeng Chen. 2020.

Gshard: Scaling giant models with conditional computation and automatic sharding. *arXiv preprint arXiv:2006.16668*.

Rui Liu, Young Jin Kim, Alexandre Muzio, and Hany Hassan. 2022. Gating dropout: Communication-efficient regularization for sparsely activated transformers. In *International Conference on Machine Learning*, pages 13782–13792. PMLR.

Samyam Rajbhandari, Conglong Li, Zhewei Yao, Minjia Zhang, Reza Yazdani Aminabadi, Ammar Ahmad Awan, Jeff Rasley, and Yuxiong He. 2022. Deepspeed-moe: Advancing mixture-of-experts inference and training to power next-generation ai scale.

Noam Shazeer, Youlong Cheng, Niki Parmar, Dustin Tran, Ashish Vaswani, Penporn Koanantakool, Peter Hawkins, HyoukJoong Lee, Mingsheng Hong, Cliff Young, et al. 2018. Mesh-tensorflow: Deep learning for supercomputers. *Advances in neural information processing systems*, 31.

Noam Shazeer, Azalia Mirhoseini, Krzysztof Maziarz, Andy Davis, Quoc Le, Geoffrey Hinton, and Jeff Dean. 2017. Outrageously large neural networks: The sparsely-gated mixture-of-experts layer. *arXiv preprint arXiv:1701.06538*.

Shaden Smith, Mostofa Patwary, Brandon Norick, Patrick LeGresley, Samyam Rajbhandari, Jared Casper, Zhun Liu, Shrimai Prabhumoye, George Zerveas, Vijay Korthikanti, Elton Zhang, Rewon Child, Reza Yazdani Aminabadi, Julie Bernauer, Xia Song, Mohammad Shoeybi, Yuxiong He, Michael Houston, Saurabh Tiwary, and Bryan Catanzaro. 2022. Using deepspeed and megatron to train megatron-turing nlg 530b, a large-scale generative language model.

Hao Wu, Patrick Judd, Xiaojie Zhang, Mikhail Isaev, and Paulius Micikevicius. 2020. Integer quantization for deep learning inference: Principles and empirical evaluation. *arXiv preprint arXiv:2004.09602*.

Barret Zoph, Irwan Bello, Sameer Kumar, Nan Du, Yanping Huang, Jeff Dean, Noam Shazeer, and William Fedus. 2022. St-moe: Designing stable and transferable sparse expert models.

Data-Efficient Autoregressive Document Retrieval for Fact Verification

James Thorne
KAIST AI
thorne@kaist.ac.kr

Abstract

Document retrieval is a core component of many knowledge-intensive natural language processing task formulations such as fact verification and question answering. Sources of textual knowledge, such as Wikipedia articles, condition the generation of answers from the models. Recent advances in retrieval use sequence-to-sequence models to incrementally predict the title of the appropriate Wikipedia page given a query. However, this method requires supervision in the form of human annotation to label which Wikipedia pages contain appropriate context. This paper introduces a distant-supervision method that does not require any annotation to train autoregressive retrievers that attain competitive R-Precision and Recall in a zero-shot setting. Furthermore we show that with task-specific supervised fine-tuning, autoregressive retrieval performance for two Wikipedia-based fact verification tasks can approach or even exceed full supervision using less than 1/4 of the annotated data indicating possible directions for data-efficient autoregressive retrieval.

1 Introduction

Conditioning answer generation on knowledge from textual sources is a common component of many well-studied natural language processing tasks. For example, in the SQuAD (Rajpurkar et al., 2016) question answering task, a passage of text is used as a source of information to generate this answer. To enable machine-reading at scale, recent studies combine retrieval with reasoning (Chen et al., 2017; Roller et al., 2021) mandating that systems select appropriate passages from a corpus, such as Wikipedia, to condition answer generation. Furthermore, tasks such as fact verification (Thorne et al., 2018; Wadden et al., 2020; Diggelmann et al., 2020) use evidence retrieved from a corpus and consider both the label and the retrieved passages for evaluation.

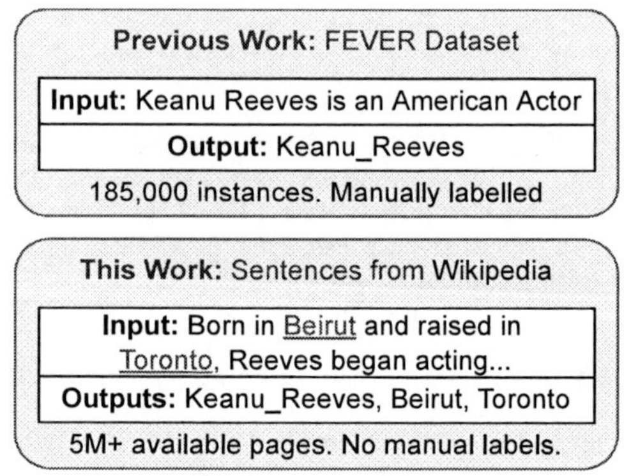

Figure 1: We present a distantly supervised pre-training objective for autoregressive information retrieval. Only using sampled sentences from Wikipedia, without labels, competitive scores can be attained for entity retrieval.

Recent advances have been made in neural retrieval models, exploiting the structure of these tasks. De Cao et al. (2020) model retrieval as entity grounding (Bunescu and Paşca, 2006; Le and Titov, 2018): the retriever is trained to predict the title of the Wikipedia document for a given input and is built on a seq2seq architecture. Even though GENRE (De Cao et al., 2020) yields improvements for many retrieval-oriented NLP tasks in the KILT benchmark (Petroni et al., 2021), the model requires supervision during training with labeled data that contains the document titles for a given input.

In this paper, we present a method for training a high-precision and high-recall retrieval system on Wikipedia data in a self-supervised manner. Our system can be trained in less than 6 hours on a single GPU without human-annotated data. The recall far exceeds conventional retrieval methods such as TF-IDF and BM25. Compared to GENRE (De Cao et al., 2020), which is trained with 11 annotated datasets for thousands of GPU-hours, our self-supervised approach for **D**ata **E**fficient

https://github.com/j6mes/sustainlp2022-deardr

Proceedings of The Third Workshop on Simple and Efficient Natural Language Processing (SustaiNLP), pages 44 - 51
December 7, 2022

Auto**R**egressive **D**ocument **R**etrieval, DEARDR, performs within an R-Precision that is 6.36% lower and a Recall@10 that is 0.91% lower for the FEVER Shared Task. We additionally show that with task-specific fine-tuning, DEARDR can attain precision and recall exceeding a fully supervised baseline for FEVER (and on-par with GENRE), with just 16K annotated instances rather than 109K in the full dataset. Similar findings are observed for the HoVer fact verification task (Jiang et al., 2020).

2 Background

Conventional information retrieval methods, such as TF-IDF and BM25, have been applied many knowledge-intensive NLP tasks (Chen et al., 2017; Thorne et al., 2018), with reasonable success. These methods do not require supervision: instead, query-document similarity is estimated based on token-level frequency information from observations on a fixed corpus. At test time, sparse discrete vector encodings of documents and the query are compared to return documents with the highest similarity to the query. While this aids application to new tasks and settings, recall can be low, especially when there are variations in phrasing due to the sparse encoding of which tokens (or variants considering n-grams or subtokens) are present. Neural retrieval (Hanselowski et al., 2018; Karpukhin et al., 2020) in contrast, uses neural networks to generate dense encodings of the query and passages. These models are trained with supervision: the training data contains lists of appropriate passages for a given query, but typically does not contain negative instances. How negative instances are sampled in training influences the suitability of the retrieved documents for the downstream task (Cohen et al., 2019; Karpukhin et al., 2020). Variants of training regimes for dense retrieval also use Cloze-task (Lee et al., 2019), Wikipedia revision information (Chang and Kao, 2012), contrastive (Izacard et al., 2021) learning, or multi-task learning (Maillard et al., 2021) to improve performance.

2.1 Autoregressive Document Retrieval

In contrast to the previous approaches, where the content of a passage is scored for a query using it's content, autoregressive document retrieval (De Cao et al., 2020) uses a seq2seq model that is trained to predict a relevant document title, such as a Wikipedia page. Tokens are decoded incrementally left to right where the and scored with $p(\mathbf{y}|\mathbf{x}) = \prod_{i=1} p(y_i|y_{<i}, \mathbf{x})$ where the decoded document title $\hat{\mathbf{y}} \in \mathcal{E}$ exists in a corpus $\mathcal{E}$. To ensure this constraint is satisfied, constrained decoding sets $p(y_i|y_{<i,x}, \mathbf{x}) = 0$ for token sequences $(y_1, \ldots y_i)$ that do not occur in the index. In practice this works well in the Wikipedia domain where document titles are simple canonical descriptors of an entity or concept. An extension, mGENRE (Cao et al., 2021), has been trained for multi-lingual entity linking using Wikipedia hyperlinks and internationalized versions of the pages from the Wikidata graph as supervision targets in other languages. This has not been applied to an entity linking task, but not evaluated for document retrieval.

Similarly, GENRE did use hyperlink-based information by incorporating data from BLINK during training. However, its contribution to system performance appears low (De Cao et al., 2020, Table 8), warranting further investigation. While the use of pre-training with hyperlink information in retrieval has shown promise (Ma et al., 2021) in other formulations, the use of distant-supervision in autoregressive retrieval, using the article titles and hyperlinks in training is emerging and has been studied in contemporaneous work (Chen et al., 2022). Lee et al. (2022) train autoregressive models for multi-hop retrieval, with a data augmentation strategy. Alternative autoregressive retrieval formulations are designed to predict document sub-strings (Bevilacqua et al., 2022): this obviates the need to have unique document identifiers.

3 Data Efficient Document Retrieval

The primary objective of this paper is to reduce the dependency on supervised instances and exploit *distant supervision* to train an autoregressive document retrieval system. Distant supervision for DEARDR exploits the structural aspects of the Wikipedia corpus: specifically, the page titles (denoted PT) and hyperlinks (denoted HL) from sentences to other pages. Sentences from Wikipedia documents are sampled from the corpus as input and DEARDR is trained to decode the page title or hyperlinks, or both (denoted PTHL).

Even though the DEARDR has only been pretrained with distant supervision without exposure to annotated training data for a knowledge intensive NLP task, we hypothesize that training to predict a Wikipedia page title or hyperlinks acts a a reasonable analog that simulates a common component of many retrieval oriented tasks. This should be sufficient to allow zero-shot application to retrieve relevant documents without the need for human annotations enabling application of knowledge-intensive NLP tasks to new domains or languages. In contrast, the GENRE model (De Cao et al., 2020) is trained with data from eleven Wikipedia-based NLP tasks with millions of annotated instances.

Constrained decoding At test time, a result set is decoded by aggregating the results from a beam search (Sutskever et al., 2014) with constrained decoding (De Cao et al., 2020). However, in contrast to GENRE, which predicts a single entity per beam, DEARDR is trained to predict a sequence of all the hyperlinked page names (illustrated in Figure 1).

Self-supervised vs task-specific retriever Once the DEARDR retriever has been pre-trained with self-supervision on Wikipedia data, it can be applied in a *zero-shot* setting to the knowledge-intensive task of fact verification. Some aspects of the test-task formulation, may have patterns that differ to what DEARDR is exposed to during the pre-training. Using small numbers of task-specific training data, the pre-trained DEARDR will be fine-tuned evaluated on downstream tasks. We hypothesize that the pre-training regimen for DEARDR will reduce the number of instances needed to train the system and attain similar performance to a system with full supervision.

4 Experimental Setup

Three different pre-training regimens for DEARDR, based on page title (PT), sentence hyperlinks (HL) and a combination of both (PTHL), are performed using the snapshot of Wikipedia from June 2017. This was the snapshot used for the FEVER shared task. Document-level retrieval for two fact verification tasks will be evaluated: FEVER (Thorne et al., 2018) and HoVER (Jiang et al., 2020).

Zero-Shot Document Retrieval: Without exposure to the underlying test task, DEARDR will be pre-trained using unlabeled instances from English Wikipedia articles (pre-trained with PT, HL or PTHL), and then applied to instances from these retrieval-based NLP tasks. From Wikipedia, we generate 16.8M distant-supervision instances.

Data-Efficient Document Retrieval: The DEARDR model will be fine-tuned using a low number of labeled instances from the target task. During training, we sample instances uniformly at random. We optimize training for *Recall* with early stopping. This occurred after 12,500 steps (100K instances in total).

Supervised Baseline: For a controlled baseline system that DEARDR can be compared against, we train a document retriever for the target task using all available data in a fully supervised setting.

Previous Work: We compare to GENRE (De Cao et al., 2020) which was trained with data from *eleven* retrieval tasks. We also compare to sparse-vector retrieval methods such as BM25 and TF-IDF. Finally, for dense-vector retrieval, we compare against DPR (Karpukhin et al., 2020). Because contrastive retrieval (Izacard et al., 2021) does not offer significant advantages over BM25 for FEVER, we do not evaluate against it.

4.1 Evaluation

Document retrieval is evaluated using two performance evaluation metrics: R-Precision and Recall@k. R-Precision is the precision of retrieved documents@R where R is the number of expected elements labeled for the instance. If the test set only specifies 1 valid document, this is equivalent to Precision@1. However, datasets sometimes require a multi-hop combination of pages for inference, requiring multiple documents to be considered for evaluation. Recall@k is the proportion of the gold documents present in the first k elements predicted by the model. This metric is a useful indicator of potential upper-bound system performance for some tasks, such as FEVER, which considers up to 5 retrieval results for scoring claim veracity. Where multiple answer sets are present for instances, we consider each answer set independently and return the max score over all the sets to allow comparison to the KILT methodology (Petroni et al., 2021).

4.2 Implementation

We use the HuggingFace (Wolf et al., 2020) implementation of T5-base (Raffel et al., 2020). This is fine-tuned using data as outlined in the previous section. We optimize hyper-parameters by sweeping the learning rate and scheduler (documented in Appendix A.2) and maximizing R-Precision on the dev split. The index for constraining decoding is constructed from all subtokens generated by the T5 Tokenizer for article titles from the Wikipedia version for the test task.

Trainer	R-Precision (%)		Recall@10 (%)	
	Page	Link	Page	Link
GENRE	*26.51*	*38.45*	*36.28*	*55.31*
PT	33.12	21.10	40.04	29.95
HL	2.65	**71.91**	17.49	84.35
PTHL	**33.17**	38.91	**37.70**	**84.89**

Table 1: R-Precision and Recall of page titles (page), and hyperlink destinations (link) of sentences sampled from Wikipedia using our training approaches (PT, HL, PTHL) compared to a contemporary supervised approach which only underwent task-specific traiing and did not undergo the pre-training.

5 Results and Discussion

5.1 Pre-training Intrinsic Evaluation

DearDr was optimized by selecting the model with the highest R-precision on the FEVER shared task. For the R-Precision on the PT and HL components of the pre-training task, we provide the following intrinsic evaluation listed in Table 1 to evaluate the pre-training objectives. Without pre-training on hyperlinks, recall is low indicating that hyperlink pre-training may be beneficial to multi-entity retrieval needed for some FEVER instances.

5.2 Downstream Extrinsic Evaluation

FEVER: For the FEVER shared task, we trained DEARDR with instances sampled from the Wikipedia snapshot for the task without using any human-annotated data. Table 2 highlights the retriever's R-Precision and Recall@10 in comparison to a fully supervised system showing that in the zero shot setting (without exposure to any labeled data) document retrieval scores are adequate and far exceed retrieval from token-based similarity methods such as TF-IDF and BM25. Because FEVER is a claim verification task, the claims are similar in nature to sentences sampled from Wikipedia pages. The similarity between the claims and the Wikipedia sentences the zero-shot system was exposed to during training mean that this system is able to apply well to this task.

While GENRE was trained on 11 tasks with over 100K fact verification instances and over 500K question answering instances, the R-Precision of our zero-shot system is only 6.36% lower with Recall@10 less than one percent lower. Given that most modern fact verification approaches perform

Approach	FEVER Retrieval (%)	
	R-Prec	Recall@10
DEARDR (PT) ZS	77.66	91.95
DEARDR (HL) ZS	56.55	89.94
DEARDR (PTHL) ZS	75.89	88.18
DEARDR (PT) 16K	82.49	**94.85**
Supervised	81.36	94.28
GENRE (11 tasks)	**84.02**	92.86
TF-IDF	29.89	68.57
BM25	40.42	70.58
DPR	55.98	77.53

Table 2: Without exposure to training instances from the FEVER task, DEARDR attains high recall and R-Precision (R-Prec) for document retrieval for FEVER in a zero-shot (ZS) setting and can be further improved with fine-tuning on 16K (16,000) data.

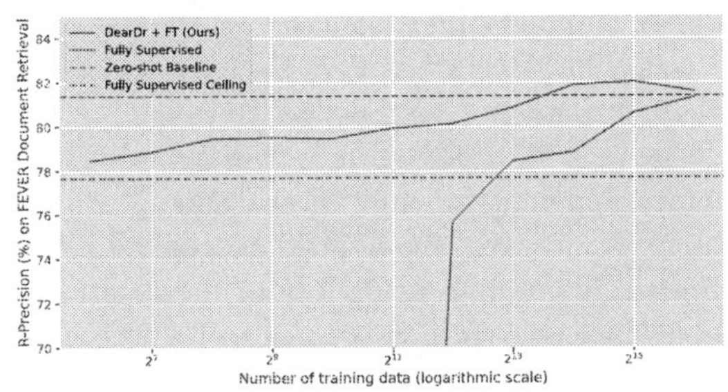

Figure 2: Learning curve showing greater R-Precision when training with fewer instances using DEARDR pre-training compared to conventional supervised training

supervised re-ranking of sentences from these documents, we do not foresee this lower precision having such a large impact on the final task score.

With full supervision from the FEVER task, our control model for comparison attains an R-Precision of 81.36%. However, with small numbers of instances for fine-tuning on FEVER, higher recalls can be attained. With 16,384 instances (less than 1/8 of the dataset), an R-Precision and Recall@10 exceeding this supervised baseline can be achieved. Furthermore, with only 2048 instances (2% of the dataset), an R-Precision of at least 80% is attained. In contrast, without pre-training R-Precision for both of these models with the same number of data is less than 30%. Learning curves are plotted in Figure 2.

HOVER: The multi-hop nature of HoVer presents more complex reasoning challenges than

Approach	HOVER Retrieval (%)	
	R-Prec	**Recall@10**
GENRE (Transfer)	43.28	49.41
DEARDR (PT) ZS	32.83	36.43
DEARDR (HL) ZS	42.22	43.78
DEARDR (PTHL) ZS	38.94	47.44
DEARDR(PTHL) 4K	45.62	49.14
DEARDR(PTHL) All	**46.23**	50.33
Supervised 4K	29.24	35.22
Supervised	46.22	**50.38**

Table 3: The multi-hop aspect of HoVer presents new challenges. Despite this, DearDr attains higher R-Prec with fewer training data than supervised baselines

FEVER and is reported in Table 3. Our zero-shot model has R-Precision that is less than 1% of GENRE. While GENRE wasn't trained on HoVer, it was trained on HotpotQA (Yang et al., 2018) which the HoVer dataset is derived from.

The benefit of pre-training with hyperlinks becomes apparent for multi-hop challenges as R-Precision for HL and PTHL exceed PT. With limited fine-tuning, using $1/4$ of the dataset, R-Precision with DEARDR is less than 1% away from a fully supervised model, despite using fewer data. Without pre-training, R-Precision is unsatisfactory. With all data, DEARDR performs as good as a model without pre-training. While DEARDR is beneficial for this task with fewer data, there are clearly more complex challenges with multi-hop reasoning that require further data augmentation, such as (Lee et al., 2022), to be solved solved by autoregressive methods for retrieval.

Question Answering: The similarity between fact verification and DEARDR pre-training is similar, aiding retrieval. However, application to question answering (TriviaQA (Joshi et al., 2017, TQA), HotpotQA (Yang et al., 2018, HPQA) and NaturalQuestions (Kwiatkowski et al., 2019, NQ)) requires further study. Table 4 shows pre-training does offer a benefit, but with fewer data for fine-tuning, similar gains in retrieval cannot be attained.

6 Conclusions and Future Work

We show that distant supervision and pre-training enables high precision autoregressive document retrieval with fewer annotated training data. While previous work has studied the utility of pre-training

Approach	R-Precision (%)		
	TQA	HPQA	NQ
GENRE*	69.2	51.3	60.3
DEARDR (PTHL) ZS	44.24	42.44	18.05
DEARDR (PTHL) 32K	53.98	43.54	36.94

Table 4: Application to question answering highlights further challenges (* reported by De Cao et al. (2020)).

for dense-retrieval, this work aids understanding of sparse autoregressive retrieval. In application to fact verification, fewer labeled training data were required. However, when we applied this method to question answering, satisfactory results were not obtained due to the domain shift between the two tasks. Better understanding this limitation would be required to adapt DEARDR pre-training to a wider range of tasks and multi-hop reasoning.

Acknowledgments

This work was supported by Institute of Information & communications Technology Planning & Evaluation (IITP) grant funded by the Korea government (MSIT) (No.2019-0-00075, Artificial Intelligence Graduate School Program (KAIST)).

References

Michele Bevilacqua, Giuseppe Ottaviano, Patrick Lewis, Wen-tau Yih, Sebastian Riedel, and Fabio Petroni. 2022. Autoregressive search engines: Generating substrings as document identifiers. *arXiv preprint arXiv:2204.10628.*

Razvan Bunescu and Marius Paşca. 2006. Using encyclopedic knowledge for named entity disambiguation. In *11th Conference of the European Chapter of the Association for Computational Linguistics*, pages 9–16, Trento, Italy. Association for Computational Linguistics.

Nicola De Cao, Ledell Wu, Kashyap Popat, Mikel Artetxe, Naman Goyal, Mikhail Plekhanov, Luke Zettlemoyer, Nicola Cancedda, Sebastian Riedel, and Fabio Petroni. 2021. Multilingual autoregressive entity linking. In *arXiv pre-print 2103.12528.*

Yang-Jui Chang and Hung-Yu Kao. 2012. Link prediction in a bipartite network using wikipedia revision information. In *2012 Conference on Technologies and Applications of Artificial Intelligence*, pages 50–55. IEEE.

Danqi Chen, Adam Fisch, Jason Weston, and Antoine Bordes. 2017. Reading Wikipedia to answer open-domain questions. In *Proceedings of the 55th Annual*

Meeting of the Association for Computational Linguistics (Volume 1: Long Papers), pages 1870–1879, Vancouver, Canada. Association for Computational Linguistics.

Jiangui Chen, Ruqing Zhang, Jiafeng Guo, Yiqun Liu, Yixing Fan, and Xueqi Cheng. 2022. Corpusbrain: Pre-train a generative retrieval model for knowledge-intensive language tasks. In *Proceedings of the 31st ACM International Conference on Information & Knowledge Management*, pages 191–200.

Daniel Cohen, Scott M. Jordan, and W. Bruce Croft. 2019. Learning a better negative sampling policy with deep neural networks for search. In *Proceedings of the 2019 ACM SIGIR International Conference on Theory of Information Retrieval*, ICTIR '19, page 19–26, New York, NY, USA. Association for Computing Machinery.

Nicola De Cao, Gautier Izacard, Sebastian Riedel, and Fabio Petroni. 2020. Autoregressive entity retrieval. In *International Conference on Learning Representations*.

Thomas Diggelmann, Jordan Boyd-Graber, Jannis Bulian, Massimiliano Ciaramita, and Markus Leippold. 2020. Climate-fever: A dataset for verification of real-world climate claims. pages 1–16.

Andreas Hanselowski, Hao Zhang, Zile Li, Daniil Sorokin, Benjamin Schiller, Claudia Schulz, and Iryna Gurevych. 2018. UKP-athene: Multi-sentence textual entailment for claim verification. In *Proceedings of the First Workshop on Fact Extraction and VERification (FEVER)*, pages 103–108, Brussels, Belgium. Association for Computational Linguistics.

Gautier Izacard, Mathilde Caron, Lucas Hosseini, Sebastian Riedel, Piotr Bojanowski, Armand Joulin, and Edouard Grave. 2021. Towards unsupervised dense information retrieval with contrastive learning. *arXiv preprint arXiv:2112.09118*.

Yichen Jiang, Shikha Bordia, Zheng Zhong, Charles Dognin, Maneesh Singh, and Mohit Bansal. 2020. HoVer: A dataset for many-hop fact extraction and claim verification. In *Findings of the Association for Computational Linguistics: EMNLP 2020*, pages 3441–3460, Online. Association for Computational Linguistics.

Mandar Joshi, Eunsol Choi, Daniel Weld, and Luke Zettlemoyer. 2017. TriviaQA: A large scale distantly supervised challenge dataset for reading comprehension. In *Proceedings of the 55th Annual Meeting of the Association for Computational Linguistics (Volume 1: Long Papers)*, pages 1601–1611, Vancouver, Canada. Association for Computational Linguistics.

Vladimir Karpukhin, Barlas Oguz, Sewon Min, Patrick Lewis, Ledell Wu, Sergey Edunov, Danqi Chen, and Wen-tau Yih. 2020. Dense passage retrieval for open-domain question answering. In *Proceedings of the 2020 Conference on Empirical Methods in Natural Language Processing (EMNLP)*, pages 6769–6781, Online. Association for Computational Linguistics.

Tom Kwiatkowski, Jennimaria Palomaki, Olivia Redfield, Michael Collins, Ankur Parikh, Chris Alberti, Danielle Epstein, Illia Polosukhin, Jacob Devlin, Kenton Lee, Kristina Toutanova, Llion Jones, Matthew Kelcey, Ming-Wei Chang, Andrew M. Dai, Jakob Uszkoreit, Quoc Le, and Slav Petrov. 2019. Natural questions: A benchmark for question answering research. *Transactions of the Association for Computational Linguistics*, 7:452–466.

Phong Le and Ivan Titov. 2018. Improving entity linking by modeling latent relations between mentions. In *Proceedings of the 56th Annual Meeting of the Association for Computational Linguistics (Volume 1: Long Papers)*, pages 1595–1604, Melbourne, Australia. Association for Computational Linguistics.

Hyunji Lee, Sohee Yang, Hanseok Oh, and Minjoon Seo. 2022. Generative multi-hop retrieval. *arXiv preprint arXiv:2204.13596*.

Kenton Lee, Ming-Wei Chang, and Kristina Toutanova. 2019. Latent retrieval for weakly supervised open domain question answering. In *Proceedings of the 57th Annual Meeting of the Association for Computational Linguistics*, pages 6086–6096, Florence, Italy. Association for Computational Linguistics.

Zhengyi Ma, Zhicheng Dou, Wei Xu, Xinyu Zhang, Hao Jiang, Zhao Cao, and Ji-Rong Wen. 2021. Pretraining for ad-hoc retrieval: hyperlink is also you need. In *Proceedings of the 30th ACM International Conference on Information & Knowledge Management*, pages 1212–1221.

Jean Maillard, Vladimir Karpukhin, Fabio Petroni, Wentau Yih, Barlas Oguz, Veselin Stoyanov, and Gargi Ghosh. 2021. Multi-task retrieval for knowledge-intensive tasks. In *Proceedings of the 59th Annual Meeting of the Association for Computational Linguistics and the 11th International Joint Conference on Natural Language Processing (Volume 1: Long Papers)*, pages 1098–1111, Online. Association for Computational Linguistics.

Fabio Petroni, Aleksandra Piktus, Angela Fan, Patrick Lewis, Majid Yazdani, Nicola De Cao, James Thorne, Yacine Jernite, Vladimir Karpukhin, Jean Maillard, Vassilis Plachouras, Tim Rocktäschel, and Sebastian Riedel. 2021. KILT: a benchmark for knowledge intensive language tasks. In *Proceedings of the 2021 Conference of the North American Chapter of the Association for Computational Linguistics: Human Language Technologies*, pages 2523–2544, Online. Association for Computational Linguistics.

Colin Raffel, Noam Shazeer, Adam Roberts, Katherine Lee, Sharan Narang, Michael Matena, Yanqi Zhou, Wei Li, and Peter J. Liu. 2020. Exploring the limits of transfer learning with a unified text-to-text transformer. *Journal of Machine Learning Research*, 21(140):1–67.

Pranav Rajpurkar, Jian Zhang, Konstantin Lopyrev, and Percy Liang. 2016. SQuAD: 100,000+ questions for machine comprehension of text. In *Proceedings of the 2016 Conference on Empirical Methods in Natural Language Processing*, pages 2383–2392, Austin, Texas. Association for Computational Linguistics.

Stephen Roller, Emily Dinan, Naman Goyal, Da Ju, Mary Williamson, Yinhan Liu, Jing Xu, Myle Ott, Eric Michael Smith, Y-Lan Boureau, and Jason Weston. 2021. Recipes for building an open-domain chatbot. In *Proceedings of the 16th Conference of the European Chapter of the Association for Computational Linguistics: Main Volume*, pages 300–325, Online. Association for Computational Linguistics.

Ilya Sutskever, Oriol Vinyals, and Quoc V Le. 2014. Sequence to sequence learning with neural networks. In *Advances in Neural Information Processing Systems*, volume 27. Curran Associates, Inc.

James Thorne, Andreas Vlachos, Christos Christodoulopoulos, and Arpit Mittal. 2018. FEVER: a large-scale dataset for fact extraction and VERification. In *Proceedings of the 2018 Conference of the North American Chapter of the Association for Computational Linguistics: Human Language Technologies, Volume 1 (Long Papers)*, pages 809–819, New Orleans, Louisiana. Association for Computational Linguistics.

David Wadden, Shanchuan Lin, Kyle Lo, Lucy Lu Wang, Madeleine van Zuylen, Arman Cohan, and Hannaneh Hajishirzi. 2020. Fact or fiction: Verifying scientific claims. In *Proceedings of the 2020 Conference on Empirical Methods in Natural Language Processing (EMNLP)*, pages 7534–7550, Online. Association for Computational Linguistics.

Thomas Wolf, Lysandre Debut, Victor Sanh, Julien Chaumond, Clement Delangue, Anthony Moi, Pierric Cistac, Tim Rault, Remi Louf, Morgan Funtowicz, Joe Davison, Sam Shleifer, Patrick von Platen, Clara Ma, Yacine Jernite, Julien Plu, Canwen Xu, Teven Le Scao, Sylvain Gugger, Mariama Drame, Quentin Lhoest, and Alexander Rush. 2020. Transformers: State-of-the-art natural language processing. In *Proceedings of the 2020 Conference on Empirical Methods in Natural Language Processing: System Demonstrations*, pages 38–45, Online. Association for Computational Linguistics.

Zhilin Yang, Peng Qi, Saizheng Zhang, Yoshua Bengio, William Cohen, Ruslan Salakhutdinov, and Christopher D. Manning. 2018. HotpotQA: A dataset for diverse, explainable multi-hop question answering. In *Proceedings of the 2018 Conference on Empirical Methods in Natural Language Processing*, pages 2369–2380, Brussels, Belgium. Association for Computational Linguistics.

A Appendix

A.1 Hardware Requirements

Experiments were performed on a single workstation with a single NVIDIA GTX 1080 Ti GPU.

A.2 Implementation

A.2.1 Pre-training

The following parameters were adjusted as part of the hyper-parameter optimization with the best parameters for all experiments indicated in bold. For HL, using learning rate of 5e-6 was more beneficial.

- Learning rate: 1e-4, **5e-5**, 1e-5, *5e-6*, 1e-6.
- Scheduler: **constant with warmup**, constant, linear.

A.2.2 Fine-tuning + Supervised

The following parameters were adjusted as part of the hyper-parameter optimization with the best parameters for all experiments indicated in bold. For fine-tuning, using a dropout of 0.2 was more beneficial.

- Learning rate: 1e-4, 5e-5, **1e-5,** 5e-6, 1e-6.
- Scheduler: **constant with warmup**, constant, linear.
- Dropout: **0.1**, 0.2, 0.3

B Licenses

The dataset released with this paper makes use of data from Wikipedia which is licensed under creative commons CC-BY-SA 4.0 license.

AfroLM: A Self-Active Learning-based Multilingual Pretrained Language Model for 23 African Languages

Bonaventure F. P. Dossou[1,2,*], **Atnafu Lambebo Tonja**[3,*], **Oreen Yousuf**[4,*], **Salomey Osei**[5,*], **Abigail Oppong**[6,*], **Iyanuoluwa Shode**[7,*], **Oluwabusayo Olufunke Awoyomi**[8,*], **Chris Chinenye Emezue**[1,9,*]

[*]Masakhane NLP, [1]Mila Quebec AI Institute, Canada, [2] McGill University, Canada, [3]Instituto Politécnico Nacional, Mexico, [4]Uppsala University, Sweden, [5]Universidad de Deusto, Spain [6]Ashesi University, Ghana, [7]Montclair State University, USA, [8]The College of Saint Rose, USA, [9]Technical University of Munich, Germany

Abstract

In recent years, multilingual pre-trained language models have gained prominence due to their remarkable performance on numerous downstream Natural Language Processing tasks (NLP). However, pre-training these large multilingual language models requires a lot of training data, which is not available for African Languages. Active learning is a semi-supervised learning algorithm, in which a model consistently and dynamically learns to identify the most beneficial samples to train itself on, in order to achieve better optimization and performance on downstream tasks. Furthermore, active learning effectively and practically addresses real-world data scarcity. Despite all its benefits, active learning, in the context of NLP and especially multilingual language models pretraining, has received little consideration. In this paper, we present **AfroLM**, a multilingual language model pretrained from scratch on 23 African languages (the largest effort to date) using our novel self-active learning framework. Pretrained on a dataset significantly (14x) smaller than existing baselines, **AfroLM** outperforms many multilingual pretrained language models (AfriBERTa, XLMR-base, mBERT) on various NLP downstream tasks (NER, text classification, and sentiment analysis). Additional out-of-domain sentiment analysis experiments show that **AfroLM** is able to generalize well across various domains. We release the code source, and our datasets used in our framework at `https://github.com/bonaventuredossou/MLM_AL`.

1 Introduction

With the appearance of Transformer models (Vaswani et al., 2017), the field of Natural Language Processing (NLP) has seen the emergence of powerful multilingual pre-trained language models (MPLMs), such as mBERT (Devlin et al., 2018), XLM-RoBERTa (XML-R) (Conneau et al., 2019), and mT5 (Xue et al., 2021). These prominent models have helped achieve state-of-the-art (SOTA) performance in many downstream NLP tasks such as named entity recognition (NER) (Alabi et al., 2022a; Adelani et al., 2021a; Devlin et al., 2018; Conneau et al., 2019), text classification (Kelechi et al., 2021), and sentiment analysis (Alabi et al., 2022a; Adelani et al., 2021a; Devlin et al., 2018; Conneau et al., 2019). However they usually require a large amount of unlabeled text corpora for good performance: mBERT was trained on Wikipedia (2,500M words) and BookCorpus (Zhu et al., 2015) (800M words) across 104 languages - 5 of which are African; mT5 supports 101 languages (13 African) and XLM-R supports 100 languages (8 African), and were trained on mC4 (Xue et al., 2021) and CommonCrawl data (Wenzek et al., 2019), respectively. This requirement for large-scale datasets contrasts sharply with the scarcity of available text corpora for African languages, which has pushed them into low-resource settings and largely excluded them from the pre-training phase of these large pre-trained models (Joshi et al., 2020; Adelani et al., 2022a). This exclusion, leads very often, to a poor performance on languages unseen during pre-training (Alabi et al., 2022a) which eventually leads to inability to carry out the required NLP task.

Active learning is a semi-supervised machine learning algorithm that makes use of only a few initial training data points to achieve better performance of a given model **M**. The optimization is done by iteratively training **M**, and using another model **N**, usually referred to as the *oracle*, to choose new training samples that will help **M** find better configurations while improving its performance (e.g., prediction accuracy). This makes active learning a prevalent paradigm to cope with data scarcity. The efficiency of active learning (i.e. its ability to produce better performance despite being trained on a smaller training data) has been proven in tasks such as biological sequence design (Jain et al., 2022), chemical sampling (Smith

Proceedings of The Third Workshop on Simple and Efficient Natural Language Processing (SustaiNLP), pages 52 - 64
December 7, 2022 ©2022 Association for Computational Linguistics

Languages	Family	Writing System	African Region	No of Speakers	Initial # of Sentences	Source	Size (MB)
Amharic (amh)	Afro-Asiatic/Semitic	Ge'ez script	East	57M	655,079	✤,✝,★	279
Afan Oromo (orm)	Afro-Asiatic/Cushitic	Latin script	East	37.4M	50,105	✝	9.87
Bambara (bam)	NC/Manding	Latin, Arabic(Ajami), N'ko	West	14M	6,618	✤	1.00
Ghomálá' (bbj)	NC/Grassfields	Latin script	Central	1M	4,841	✤	0.50
Éwé (ewe)	NC/Kwa	Latin (Ewe alphabet)	West	7M	5,615	✤	0.50
Fon (fon)	NC/Volta-Niger	Latin script	West	1.7M	5,448	✤	1.00
Hausa (hau)	Afro-Asiatic/Chadic	Latin (Boko alphabet)	West	63M	1,626,330	✤,✝,★	208
Igbo (ibo)	NC/Volta-Niger	Latin (Önwu alphabet)	West	27M	437,737	✤,✝,★	63
Kinyarwanda (kin)	NC/Rwanda-Rundi	Latin script	Central	9.8M	84,994	➻,✝,✤	37.70
Lingala (lin)	NC/Bang	Latin script	Central & East	45M	398,440	✤	45.90
Luganda (lug)	NC/Bantu	Latin script (Ganda alphabet)	East	7M	74,754	✝,✤	8.34
Luo (luo)	Nilo-Saharan	Latin script	East	4M	8,684	✝	1.29
Mooré (mos)	NC/Gur	Latin script	West	8M	27,908	✤,✝	5.05
Chewa (nya)	NC/Nyasa	Latin script	South & East	12M	8,000	✤	1.66
Naija (pcm)	English-Creole	Latin script	West	75M	345,694	✤,✝,★	101
Shona (sna)	NC/Bantu	Latin script (Shona alphabet)	Southeast	12M	187,810	✤,✝	32.80
Swahili (swa)	NC / Bantu	Latin script (Roman Swahili alphabet)	East & Central	98M	1,935,485	✤,✝,★	276
Setswana (tsn)	NC / Bantu	Latin (Tswana alphabet)	South	14M	13,958	✤,✝	2.21
Akan/Twi (twi)	NC / Kwa	Latin script	West	9M	14,701	✤	1.61
Wolof (wol)	NC / Senegambia	Latin (Wolof alphabet)	West	5M	13,868	✝	2.20
Xhosa (xho)	NC/Zunda	Latin (Xhosa alphabet)	South	20M	93,288	✤,✝	17.40
Yorùbá (yor)	NC / Volta-Niger	Latin (Yorùbá alphabet)	West	42M	290,999	✤,✝,★	45.9
isiZulu (zul)	NC / Bantu	Latin (Zulu alphabet)	South	27M	194,562	✤,✝	33.70

Table 1: **Languages Corpora Details. Legends**: (Adelani et al., 2022a) → ✤, (Alabi et al., 2022a) → ✝, (Kelechi et al., 2021) → ★, (Niyongabo et al., 2020) → ➻.

et al., 2018), and Deep Bayesian (DB) approaches on image data (Gal et al., 2017). Also, most of the work on deep active learning focuses on image classification with Convolutional Neural Networks (CNNs). It should be noted that active learning has been greatly explored and used to perform classification tasks, but not in language generation and understanding, and this is what we hope to address.

A study of active learning in the context of NLP has been carried out by (Siddhant and Lipton, 2018). In their study, it is shown that active learning with DB networks coupled with uncertainty measures and acquisition function outperforms several i.i.d baselines. They showed that with only 20% of samples labeled, their approach reached an accuracy of 98-99% on the Named Entity Recognition (NER) task, while i.i.d tasks required 50% of labelled data to achieve comparable performance. In their study on clinical texts, (Chen et al., 2015) also proved that active learning algorithms outperformed other learning methods. (Ein-Dor et al., 2020; Tonneau et al., 2022) on their works with BERT model(s) (for n different languages, there were n different BERT-based models) went further by showing that active learning works with a balanced and unbalanced dataset. They also showed that the different active learning methods performed relatively the same.

In our work, we fixed **M=N** (hence the title **self-active learning**). In our framework, we give **M** the ability to query itself, and use the knowledge acquired during each active learning round to construct new data points (from existing ones) that will be used for the next active learning round.

We considered a diverse set of 23 African languages spread across the African continent. The selected languages are spoken in the south, central, east, and western regions of Africa. The languages cover four language families: Afro-Asiatic (e.g., Amharic, Hausa, Afan Omoro), Niger-Congo (NC) (e.g., Yorùbá, Bambara, Fon), English-Creole (Naija) and Nilo-Saharan (Luo) (see Appendix A for details). For each language, a dataset was collected from the news domain, which encompassed many topics such as health, politics, society, sport, environment, etc.

Our primary contribution to this work is our proposal of a **self-active learning framework** in which we pre-train the **biggest Multilingual African Language Model** (for the number of languages covered) to date, and we show that our setup is **very data-efficient and provides improvements** on downstream NLP tasks such as NER, text classification, and sentiment analysis (even on out-of-domain experiments).

2 Related Works on MPLMs for African Languages

Language adaptive fine-tuning (LAFT) is one of the best approaches to adapt MPLMs to a new language. This entails fine-tuning an MPLM on monolingual texts of the said language with the same pre-training objective. However, this cannot be efficiently applied to African languages facing data-scarcity. (Alabi et al., 2022b) proposed a new adaptation method called *Multilingual adaptive fine-tuning (MAFT)*, as an approach to adapt MPLMs to many African languages with a single

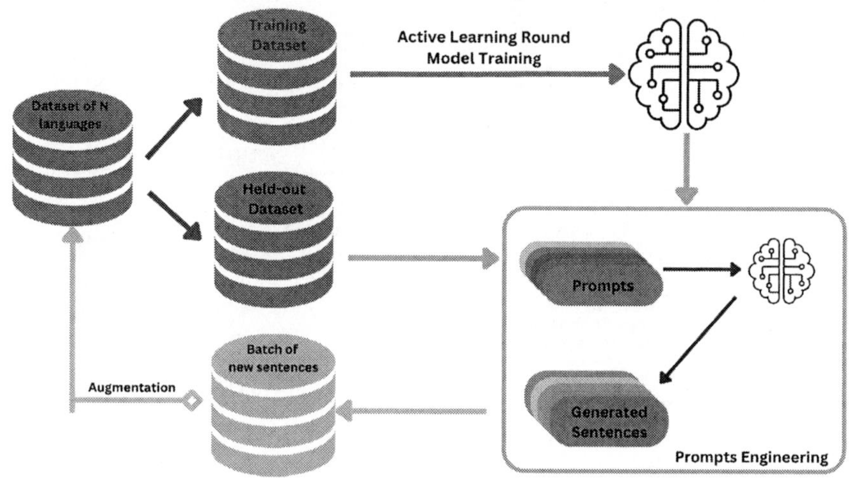

Figure 1: Self-Active Learning Framework). The process is designed in 4 stages (fully explained and detailed in Algorithm 1): (1) ■ Dataset split for current Active Learning round, (2) ■ Active Learning round training, (3) ■ Generation of new sentence samples for the current round, and (4) ■ Augmentation of the datasets of all languages.

model. Their results show that MAFT is competitive to LAFT while providing a single model rather than many models that are specific for individual languages. Nevertheless, Alabi et al. (2022b)'s approach still works under the assumption that one does not need to train a model from scratch for languages in the low-resource settings, as they could benefit from high-resource languages. We find that this is not *always* the case.

(Kelechi et al., 2021) introduced AfriBERTa, a multilingual language model trained on less than 1GB of data from 11 African languages. Training AfriBERTa from scratch showcased how African languages can benefit from being included in the pre-training stage of MPLMs. AfriBERTa produced competitive results compared to existing MPLMs (e.g., mBERT, XLM-R), and outperformed them on text classification and NER tasks. Rather than relying on high-resource languages for transfer-learning, AfriBERTa leverages the linguistic similarity between languages with low-resource settings to produce promising results. (Kelechi et al., 2021) empirically demonstrates that this is more beneficial to these languages and is crucial in assessing the viability of language models pretrained on small datasets.

(Antoine and Niyongabo, 2022) went beyond the linguistic taxonomy in creating KinyaBERT, a morphology-aware language model for Kinyarwanda. Trained on a 2.4GB corpus containing news articles from 370 websites registered between 2011 and 2021, KinyaBERT boasts a Transformer-like architecture that helps the representation of morphological compositionality. Their experiments outperformed solid baseline results for tasks such as NER and machine-translated GLUE on the Kinyarwanda language. These results demonstrated the effectiveness of not relying on transfer learning from high resource languages and rather explicitly incorporating morphological information of the African languages in their pretraining stage.

In the next section, we will describe our self-active learning framework, and the core details of our approach.

3 Self-Active Learning Framework

In this section, we describe our self-active learning framework (Figure 1). In Algorithm 1, we present a single active learning loop. In our current work, our model is trained only with a Masked Language Modeling (MLM) objective (Conneau et al., 2019; Conneau and Lample, 2019; Devlin et al., 2018). We plan to further incorporate Translation Language Modeling (TLM) objective to improve translations of low-resource languages with relatively few thousands of data points [1]. This will be useful for both supervised and unsupervised translation (Adelani et al., 2022a; Conneau et al., 2019).

We used a shared Sentence Piece vocabulary with 250, 000 BPE codes. The subword shared

[1] https://github.com/facebookresearch/XLM

vocabulary intends to improve alignment in the embedding space across languages (see languages description in Appendix A and corpora details in Table 1) that are linguistically similar in features such as script/alphabet, morphology, etc. (Conneau et al., 2019), reflecting our focus languages. Additionally, (Conneau et al., 2019) showed that scaling the size of the shared vocabulary (e.g. from 36,000 to 256,000) improved the performance of multilingual models on downstream tasks. Our vocabulary is defined jointly across all 23 languages and fixed during training, as opposed to random training and held-out dataset selection at each active learning round.

The motivations behind the randomness in the selection of the training and held-out datasets are: (1) to make efficient use of the limited dataset we have, and (2) to expose the model step by step, instead of simultaneously, to a variety of samples across different news sub-domains. We believe this would help in domain-shift adaptation and the robustness of the model.

As extensively detailed in Algorithm 1, at each round we randomly select m sentences per language, from the held-out dataset of the language. For a language, to generate a new sentence s', given an original sentence s, we proceed as follows (more details can be found in Algorithm 1):

1. select an initial ordered (left to right) set of words from s as prompt,
2. add a mask token at the end of the ordered set or sequence of words,
3. query the model to predict the masked token,
4. choose the best word, add it to the prompt,
5. repeat 2-4 until we reach the length of s.

The process described above will produce m new data points that will be added to the language dataset. The new dataset obtained is used to re-train the model from scratch at the next active learning round.

Algorithm 1 Self-Active Learning Training Round

Require:
- Masked Language Modeling (MLM) objective π_θ with masking probability $p = 0.15$
- Vocabulary $\mathcal{V}$, Model $\mathcal{M}$, Tokenizer $\mathcal{T}$
- Set of languages $\mathcal{L} = \bigcup_{i \in [1,23]} \{l\}$
- Overall Dataset $\mathcal{D} = \bigcup_{l \in \mathcal{L}} \mathcal{D}_l$ with $\mathcal{D}_l$ the dataset of language l
- Training Dataset $\mathcal{D}_t$ with $k\%$ randomly selected sentences from $\mathcal{D}_l, l \in \mathcal{L}$
- Held-out Dataset $\mathcal{H}$ with $1 - k\%$ samples for each language: $\mathcal{H} = \bigcup_{l \in L} \mathcal{H}_l$
- proportion t of words to successively mask in a sentence (from left to right)

Ensure:
- Initialize $\mathcal{M}$, and $\mathcal{T}$ with $\mathcal{V}$
- $k \leftarrow 80$
- $t \leftarrow 15$
- Train $\mathcal{M}$ with policy π_θ

Generate set $\mathcal{G}_l$ of new samples for each language:

```
for l ∈ L do
    G_l ← {}
    • Build S_l with m = |H_l| sentences randomly chosen from H_l    ▷ we choose m this way to cope with small size datasets
    for s ∈ S_l do
        n ← len(s), s = ⋃_{i∈[1,n]} {w_i}
        t_s ← ⌈(n*t)/100⌉ + 1
        prompt ← ⋃_{i∈[1,n−t_s]} {w_i}
        while t_s ≠ 0 do
            prompt ← prompt ∪ {<mask>}
            w_p ← M(prompt):    ▷ predicted masked word
            prompt ← prompt ∪ {w_p}
            t_s ← t_s − 1
        end while
        G_l ← G_l ∪ {prompt}
    end for
    D_l ← D_l ∪ G_l    ▷ new samples added to the language dataset
end for
```

4 Experiments, Results and Discussion

Experiments: We use the XLM-RoBERTa (XLM-R) architecture in our experiments based on previous works utilizing the model to achieve state-of-the-art performance in various downstream tasks. Following the work and results of (Kelechi et al., 2021), we trained XLM-R-based models

Model	Hyper-parameters	Values
AfroLM-Large	sequence maximum length	256
	hidden size	768
	attention heads	6
	hidden layers	10
	learning rate	1e-4
	batch size	32
	# of Parameters	264M
	total initial training examples	5,137,026
	vocabulary size	250,000
	gradient accumulation steps	8
	warming steps	40,000
	training steps	500,000

Table 2: Hyper-parameters summary

from scratch. In our current work we trained the model with 3 self-active learning rounds (we stopped at 3 due to computational resources). We used 80% and 20% of languages data for the training and held-out datasets respectively. We designed 2 versions of AfroLM: *AfroLM-Large (without self-active learning)* and *AfroLM-Large (with self-active learning)* with the hyper-parameters specified in Table 2. All training experiments were done using the HuggingFace Transformers library (Wolf et al., 2019).

Afro (without self-active learning) is one of our baselines. We trained an XLM-R model on the entire dataset, and the held-out dataset was just used for evaluation. For **AfroLM-Large** models, we used Google Cloud with a single 48GB NVIDIA A100 GPU. An active learning round took $\approx$ 260 hours of training. We evaluated **AfroLM-Large** models on three downstream tasks:

- **NER**: we evaluated the performance of our model pre-trained using our self-active learning framework on the MasakhaNER dataset (Adelani et al., 2021a). The dataset contains ten African languages: Amharic, Hausa, Igbo, Kinyarwanda, Luganda, Luo, Nigerian Pidgin, Swahili, Wolof, and Yorùbá. (Adelani et al., 2021a; Alabi et al., 2022a) also provided strong baselines with pre-trained language models like mBERT and XLM-R on MasakhaNER.

- **Text Classification**: we tested our models on Hausa and Yorùbá news text classification dataset from (Hedderich et al., 2020), where the authors have also built strong baselines on mBERT and XLM-R models.

- **Sentiment Analysis**: we tested the the out-of-domain performance of our model in two domains different from news:

  1. `Movies`: we directly fine-tuned and evaluated **AfroLM-Large** on the YOSM dataset (Shode et al., 2022), which contains reviews of Yorùbá movies.
  2. `Twitter` $\rightarrow$ `Movies`: in this setup, we finetuned on the training and validation set of NaijaSenti (Muhammad et al., 2022), and evaluated on YOSM. NaijaSenti contains human annotated tweets in Hausa, Yoruba, Igbo and Nigerian Pidgin. However, we were not able to evaluate **AfroLM-Large** on it because the authors have not yet released the test set.

Results & Discussion: Tables 1 and 3 show that our framework includes a large variety of African Languages. Table 4, and Table 5 (with 11 additional languages from MasakhaNER 2.0 dataset (Adelani et al., 2022b)) show the results of our method in comparison with other baselines on NER task. We can notice that **AfroLM-Large (w/ AL)** outperforms AfriBERTa-Large, mBERT and XLMR-base ($\approx$ 2.5 TB of data); while being pre-trained on significantly smaller dataset ($\approx$ 0.73 GB (80% of 0.91 GB initial dataset)). AfriBERTa-Large has been pretrained from scratch on 11 African languages, while mBERT and XLMR-base (with existing pretrained weights) were finetuned on the MasakhaNER dataset.

Table 6, and Table 7 show that, on the text classification, and sentiment analysis tasks, our method outperforms many existing baselines. Additionally, out-of-domain experiments and analyses show that our method is robust and provides good results in out-of-domain settings.

While AfroXLMR-base in average, slightly outperforms our approach, it is important to notice that it has been pretrained on a dataset 14x bigger than our set. Furthermore, **AfroLM-Large** has been trained on $\approx$ 0.73 GB of data (80% of 0.91 GB initial dataset), which is less than the size of the corpus used to train AfriBERTa (0.939 GB). This allows us to confidently affirm that our approach is data-efficient, while being very competitive.

It is important to note that the margin of performance from **AfroLM-Large (w/ AL)** does not come from the fact that it has been trained on more languages. Our results show that **AfroLM-Large (w/ AL)** outperforms models trained on significantly larger datasets and number of languages.

Language	In AfriBERTa?	In AfroLM?	In AfroXLMR	In mBERT?	In XLMR?
amh	✓	✓	✓	✗	✓
hau	✓	✓	✓	✗	✓
ibo	✓	✓	✓	✗	✗
kin	✓	✓	✓	✗	✗
lug	✗	✓	✗	✗	✗
luo	✗	✓	✗	✗	✗
pcm	✓	✓	✓	✗	✗
swa	✓	✓	✓	✓	✓
wol	✓	✓	✓	✗	✗
yor	✓	✓	✓	✓	✗

Table 3: Information about languages included in each language model. We can notice that AfroLM includes the most of them.

Language	AfriBERTa-Large	AfroLM-Large (w/o AL)	AfroLM-Large (w/ AL)	AfroXLMR-base	mBERT	XLMR-base
amh	73.82	43.78	**73.84**	*76.10*	00.00	70.96
hau	90.17	84.14	**91.09**	*91.10*	87.34	87.44
ibo	87.38	80.24	**87.65**	*87.40*	85.11	84.51
kin	73.78	67.56	**72.84**	*78.00*	70.98	73.93
lug	78.85	72.94	**80.38**	*82.90*	80.56	80.71
luo	70.23	57.03	**75.60**	*75.10*	72.65	75.14
pcm	85.70	73.23	**87.05**	*89.60*	87.78	87.39
swa	87.96	74.89	**87.67**	*88.60*	86.37	87.55
wol	61.81	53.58	**65.80**	*67.40*	66.10	64.38
yor	81.32	73.23	**79.37**	*82.10*	78.64	77.58
avg	79.10	68.06	**80.13**	*81.90*	71.55	79.16
avg (excl. amh)	79.69	70.76	**80.83**	*82.54*	79.50	80.07

Table 4: **NER Performances:** F1-scores on languages test sets after 50 epochs averaged over 5 seeds. These results cover all 4 tags in the MasakhaNER dataset: **PER**, **ORG**, **LOC**, **DATE**. XLM-R and mBERT results obtained from (Adelani et al., 2021b). **AfroLM-Large (w/ AL)** outperforms AfriBERTa, and the initial MasakhaNER baselines. **The bold numbers represent the performance of the model with the lowest pretrained data**. AfroXMLR-base = XLMR-Large + MAFT (Alabi et al., 2022a) with 272M parameters. MAFT gives similar performance to individual LAFT models (Alabi et al., 2022a) (LAFT results in single model per language).

Moreover, the comparison of **AfroLM-Large (w/ AL)** to **AfroLM-Large (w/o AL)** shows a significant improvement in performance, which implies that our self-active learning framework is efficient, and leads to a better performance. This is expected, because the idea of our self-active learning (and of active learning in general) is to have **AfroLM**, to consistently and dynamically, during the training phase, identify the most beneficial sample(s) to learn from in order to boost the performance.

In our current algorithm, a sentence sample is generated by ***iterative next-token prediction***: the generated sentence is the result of the concatenation of each best token. Diversity in sample generation and selection is paramount, and we believe, could improve the performance of our framework. In the limitation section (section 6), we proposed a way of selecting *diverse* sentences (after sentence generation). We also proposed a new weighted loss, that we believe will be more balanced across the entire dataset.

5 Future works and Conclusion

In conclusion, we propose **AfroLM**, a self-active learning-based multilingual language model supporting 23 African Languages; the largest to date. Our language datasets are collected from the news domain and span across different parts of the African continent. Our experimental results on NLP downstream tasks (NER, text classification, and out-of-domain sentiment analysis), prove the data-efficiency of **AfroLM** (as it has been trained on a dataset 14x smaller than its competitors), and its competitiveness as it outperforms many MPLMs (AfriBERTa, mBERT, XLMR-base) while being very competitive to *AfroXLMR-base*. We

Model	bam	bbj	ewe	fon	mos	nya	sna	tsn	twi	xho	zul	AVG
MPLMs pre-trained on from scratch on African Languages												
AfriBERTa-Large	78.60	71.00	86.90	79.90	71.40	88.60	92.40	83.20	75.70	85.00	81.70	81.31
AfroLM-Large (w/ AL)	**80.40**	**72.91**	**88.14**	**80.48**	**72.14**	**90.25**	**94.46**	**85.38**	**77.89**	**87.50**	**86.31**	**83.26**
MPLMs adapted to African Languages												
AfroXLMR-base	*79.60*	*73.30*	*89.20*	*82.30*	*74.40*	*91.90*	*95.70*	*87.70*	*78.90*	*88.60*	*88.40*	*84.55*
mBERT	78.90	60.60	86.90	79.90	71.40	88.60	92.40	86.40	75.70	85.00	81.70	80.68
XLMR-base	78.70	72.30	88.50	81.90	72.70	89.90	93.60	86.10	78.70	87.00	84.60	83.09

Table 5: **NER Baselines on MasakhaNER2.0 (Adelani et al., 2022b)**. We compare MPLMs trained from scratch on African languages, and MPLMs adapted to African Languages. The average of scores are over 5 runs. The bold numbers represent the performance of the model with the lowest pretrained data.

Language	In AfriBERTa?	In AfroLM?	AfriBERTa-Large	AfroLM-Large (w/o AL)	AfroLM-Large (w/ AL)
hau	✓	✓	90.86	85.57	**91.00**
yor	✓	✓	*83.22*	75.30	**82.90**

Table 6: **Text Classification Performances:** F1-scores on the languages test sets. **The bold numbers represent the performance of the model with the lowest pretrained data**.

Models	Yoruba F1-score
AfroLM-Large (w/o AL)	
Movies	83.12
Twitter → Movies	41.28
AfroLM-Large (w/ AL)	
Movies	**85.40**
Twitter → Movies	**68.70**
AfriBERTa-Large	
Movies	82.70
Twitter → Movies	65.90

Table 7: **Out-Of-Domain Sentiment Analysis Performance:** F1-scores on YOSM test set after 20 epochs averaged over 5 seeds. **The bold numbers represent the performance of the model with the lowest pretrained data**.

also show that **AfroLM** is also able to generalize across various domains. For future work, we intend to: (1) explore and understand the relationship between the number of active learning steps and the MPLMs performance on downstream tasks, and (2) integrate a new weighted loss, and more diversity in new data points generation and selection as we explained in the limitation section (see section 6). Our datasets, and source code are publicly available at https://github.com/bonaventuredossou/MLM_AL.

6 Limitations and Approach of Solution

Currently, the loss of the model across the training dataset (across all 23 languages), appears to be the average of the individual (cross-entropy) losses. Due to the disparate sizes of our corpora per language, the training will be biased toward the languages whose sizes predominate the training set. Therefore, we suggest a strategy to re-weight the cross entropy loss per language by the ratio of the size of the dataset for that language to the size of the entire training set:

$$\mathcal{L} = \frac{1}{N}\sum_{l}|\frac{\mathcal{D}_l}{\mathcal{D}}|\mathcal{L}_l$$

where $|\frac{\mathcal{D}_l}{\mathcal{D}}|$ is the weight of the training dataset of the language l, $\mathcal{L}_l$ is the loss of the model on a given language l, and N is the total number of languages (23 in our case). We believe this adjusts well overall loss, by using the right weighted loss of each language, that can be seen as their respective contribution to the general loss.

Another limitation of our current framework is that the samples that are generated from prompts might not be diverse. Given a batch $\mathcal{B}$ of generated samples, and a set $\mathcal{S}$ of initial samples, we want the samples selected to be substantially different from the majority of samples present in $\mathcal{S}$. We think that performing the following two steps will help to ensure this:

1. increase the number of words, in a sentence, to be masked: this implies that the length of the prompt is shortened, and that we provide less (or short) context in the input to our model. Long-range semantics is still a challenge in natural language generation and understanding, and large language models (GPT-2, DialoGPT) have insufficiently learned the effect of distant words on next-token prediction (Malkin et al., 2022). Therefore, we believe that providing a short context will increase the choices of the model and lead to the generation of more various tokens. This has been shown by (Malkin et al., 2022) where they also introduced the *coherence boosting* approach to increase the focus of a language model on a long context.

2. use the Word Error Rate (WER) as a simple diversity measurement. The WER is an adaptation of the Levenshtein distance (also called edit distance), working at the word level instead of the phoneme level. Ideally, we want high WER. Let $W = \bigcup_{i\in[1,t_s]}\{w_i\}$, the set of words from a sentence s that we cut off for the next-token prediction loop described in section 3 and in Algorithm 1. Let $W' = \bigcup_{i\in[1,t_s]}\{w'_i\}$, the set of words predicted by the model. Then, for a pair (s, s') of the original sentence and new generated sentence ($s' = prompt \cup W'$), we can define a diversity score $d_{s,s'} = WER(W, W')$. Given the definition of d, for a language l, we can define a diverse batch

$$B^l_{diverse} = \bigcup_{i\in[1,|\mathcal{H}_l|]} \{s'_i \mid d_{s_i,s'_i} \geq t\}$$

where t is an hyper-parameter, representing an error threshold. t can be tuned because a small t will result in a less diverse batch, while a very huge value will result in an empty or almost empty batch.

7 Ethics Statement

As any modern technology, machine learning algorithms, are subject to potential dual good or bad usage. Our work is motivated by the desire of making AI (in general, NLP in particular) applications to be inclusive to the low-resourced languages (which are the vast majority of existing living languages), hence benefiting to humanity and society. We strongly discourage bad and unethical use of our work (and its derivations).

References

David Ifeoluwa Adelani, Jade Abbott, Graham Neubig, Daniel D'souza, Julia Kreutzer, Constantine Lignos, Chester Palen-Michel, Happy Buzaaba, Shruti Rijhwani, Sebastian Ruder, Stephen Mayhew, Israel Abebe Azime, Shamsuddeen H. Muhammad, Chris Chinenye Emezue, Joyce Nakatumba-Nabende, Perez Ogayo, Aremu Anuoluwapo, Catherine Gitau, Derguene Mbaye, Jesujoba Alabi, Seid Muhie Yimam, Tajuddeen Rabiu Gwadabe, Ignatius Ezeani, Rubungo Andre Niyongabo, Jonathan Mukiibi, Verrah Otiende, Iroro Orife, Davis David, Samba Ngom, Tosin Adewumi, Paul Rayson, Mofetoluwa Adeyemi, Gerald Muriuki, Emmanuel Anebi, Chiamaka Chukwuneke, Nkiruka Odu, Eric Peter Wairagala, Samuel Oyerinde, Clemencia Siro, Tobius Saul Bateesa, Temilola Oloyede, Yvonne Wambui, Victor Akinode, Deborah Nabagereka, Maurice Katusiime, Ayodele Awokoya, Mouhamadane MBOUP, Dibora Gebreyohannes, Henok Tilaye, Kelechi Nwaike, Degaga Wolde, Abdoulaye Faye, Blessing Sibanda, Orevaoghene Ahia, Bonaventure F. P. Dossou, Kelechi Ogueji, Thierno Ibrahima DIOP, Abdoulaye Diallo, Adewale Akinfaderin, Tendai Marengereke, and Salomey Osei. 2021a. MasakhaNER: Named Entity Recognition for African Languages. *Transactions of the Association for Computational Linguistics*, 9:1116–1131.

David Ifeoluwa Adelani, Jade Abbott, Graham Neubig, Daniel D'souza, Julia Kreutzer, Constantine Lignos, Chester Palen-Michel, Happy Buzaaba, Shruti Rijhwani, Sebastian Ruder, et al. 2021b. Masakhaner: Named entity recognition for african languages. *Transactions of the Association for Computational Linguistics*, 9:1116–1131.

David Ifeoluwa Adelani, Jesujoba Oluwadara Alabi, Angela Fan, Julia Kreutzer, Xiaoyu Shen, Machel Reid, Dana Ruiter, Dietrich Klakow, Peter Nabende, Ernie Chang, Tajuddeen Gwadabe, Freshia Sackey, Bonaventure F. P. Dossou, Chris Chinenye Emezue, Colin Leong, Michael Beukman, Shamsuddeen Hassan Muhammad, Guyo Dub Jarso, Oreen Yousuf, Andre Niyongabo Rubungo, Gilles HACHEME, Eric Peter Wairagala, Muhammad Umair Nasir, Benjamin Ayoade Ajibade, Oluwaseyi Ajayi Ajayi, Yvonne Wambui Gitau, Jade Abbott, Mohamed Ahmed, Millicent Ochieng, Anuoluwapo Aremu, Perez Ogayo, Jonathan Mukiibi, Fatoumata Ouoba Kabore, Godson Koffi KALIPE, Derguene Mbaye, Allahsera Auguste Tapo, Victoire Memdjokam Koagne, Edwin Munkoh-Buabeng, Valencia Wagner, Idris Abdulmumin, and Ayodele Awokoya. 2022a. A few thousand translations go a long way! leveraging pre-trained models for african news translation. In *NAACL-HLT*.

David Ifeoluwa Adelani, Graham Neubig, Sebastian Ruder, Shruti Rijhwani, Michael Beukman, Chester Palen-Michel, Constantine Lignos, Jesujoba O. Alabi, Shamsuddeen H. Muhammad, Peter Nabende, Cheikh M. Bamba Dione, Andiswa Bukula, Rooweither Mabuya, Bonaventure F. P. Dossou, Blessing Sibanda, Happy Buzaaba, Jonathan Mukiibi, Godson Kalipe, Derguene Mbaye, Amelia Taylor, Fatoumata Kabore, Chris Chinenye Emezue, Anuoluwapo Aremu, Perez Ogayo, Catherine Gitau, Edwin Munkoh-Buabeng, Victoire M. Koagne, Allahsera Auguste Tapo, Tebogo Macucwa, Vukosi Marivate, Elvis Mboning, Tajuddeen Gwadabe, Tosin Adewumi, Orevaoghene Ahia, Joyce Nakatumba-Nabende, Neo L. Mokono, Ignatius Ezeani, Chiamaka Chukwuneke, Mofetoluwa Adeyemi, Gilles Q. Hacheme, Idris Abdulmumin, Odunayo Ogundepo, Oreen Yousuf, Tatiana Moteu Ngoli, and Dietrich Klakow. 2022b. Masakhaner 2.0: Africa-centric transfer learning for named entity recognition.

Jesujoba O Alabi, David Ifeoluwa Adelani, Marius Mosbach, and Dietrich Klakow. 2022a. Multilingual language model adaptive fine-tuning: A study on african languages. *arXiv preprint arXiv:2204.06487*.

Jesujoba O Alabi, Adelani David Ifeoluwa, Mosbach Marius, and Klakow Dietrich. 2022b. Multilingual Language Model Adaptive Fine-Tuning: A case study on African Languages. *COLING*.

Nzeyimana Antoine and Rubungo Andre Niyongabo. 2022. KinyaBERT:a Morphology-aware Kinyarwanda Language Model. *ACL*.

Hounkpati B. C. Capo. 1991. *A comparative phonology of Gbe*. Foris Publications.

Yukun Chen, Thomas A. Lasko, Qiaozhu Mei, Joshua C. Denny, and Hua Xu. 2015. A study of active learning methods for named entity recognition in clinical text. *Journal of Biomedical Informatics*, 58:11–18.

Alexis Conneau, Kartikay Khandelwal, Naman Goyal, Vishrav Chaudhary, Guillaume Wenzek, Francisco Guzmán, Edouard Grave, Myle Ott, Luke Zettlemoyer, and Veselin Stoyanov. 2019. Unsupervised cross-lingual representation learning at scale. *arXiv preprint arXiv:1911.02116*.

Alexis Conneau and Guillaume Lample. 2019. Cross-lingual language model pretraining. In *Advances in Neural Information Processing Systems*, volume 32. Curran Associates, Inc.

Jacob Devlin, Ming-Wei Chang, Kenton Lee, and Kristina Toutanova. 2018. Bert: Pre-training of deep bidirectional transformers for language understanding. *arXiv preprint arXiv:1810.04805*.

David M. Eberhard, Gary F. Simons, and Charles D. Fennig (eds.). 2020. Ethnologue: Languages of the world. twenty-third edition.

Liat Ein-Dor, Alon Halfon, Ariel Gera, Eyal Shnarch, Lena Dankin, Leshem Choshen, Marina Danilevsky, Ranit Aharonov, Yoav Katz, and Noam Slonim. 2020. Active Learning for BERT: An Empirical Study. In *Proceedings of the 2020 Conference on Empirical Methods in Natural Language Processing (EMNLP)*, pages 7949–7962, Online. Association for Computational Linguistics.

Yarin Gal, Riashat Islam, and Zoubin Ghahramani. 2017. Deep bayesian active learning with image data. In *Proceedings of the 34th International Conference on Machine Learning - Volume 70*, ICML'17, page 1183–1192. JMLR.org.

Michael A. Hedderich, David Adelani, Dawei Zhu, Jesujoba Alabi, Udia Markus, and Dietrich Klakow. 2020. Transfer learning and distant supervision for multilingual transformer models: A study on African languages. In *Proceedings of the 2020 Conference on Empirical Methods in Natural Language Processing (EMNLP)*, pages 2580–2591, Online. Association for Computational Linguistics.

Moksh Jain, Emmanuel Bengio, Alex-Hernandez Garcia, Jarrid Rector-Brooks, Bonaventure F. P. Dossou, Chanakya Ekbote, Jie Fu, Tianyu Zhang, Micheal Kilgour, Dinghuai Zhang, Lena Simine, Payel Das, and Yoshua Bengio. 2022. Biological sequence design with gflownets.

Pratik Joshi, Sebastin Santy, Amar Budhiraja, Kalika Bali, and Monojit Choudhury. 2020. The state and fate of linguistic diversity and inclusion in the NLP world. In *Proceedings of the 58th Annual Meeting of the Association for Computational Linguistics*, pages 6282–6293, Online. Association for Computational Linguistics.

Ogueji Kelechi, Zhu Yuxin, and Lin Jimmy. 2021. Small Data? No Problem! Exploring the Viability of Pretrained Multilingual Language Models for Low-resourced Languages. *EMNLP*, pages 116–126.

Claire Lefebvre and Anne-Marie Brousseau. 2002. *A grammar of Fongbe*. Mouton de Gruyter.

Nikolay Malkin, Zhen Wang, and Nebojsa Jojic. 2022. Coherence boosting: When your pretrained language model is not paying enough attention. In *Proceedings of the 60th Annual Meeting of the Association for Computational Linguistics (Volume 1: Long Papers)*, pages 8214–8236, Dublin, Ireland. Association for Computational Linguistics.

Shamsuddeen Hassan Muhammad, David Ifeoluwa Adelani, Sebastian Ruder, Ibrahim Said Ahmad, Idris Abdulmumin, Bello Shehu Bello, Monojit Choudhury, Chris Chinenye Emezue, Saheed Salahudeen Abdullahi, Anuoluwapo Aremu, Alipio Jeorge, and Pavel Brazdil. 2022. Naijasenti: A nigerian twitter sentiment corpus for multilingual sentiment analysis.

Rubungo Andre Niyongabo, Qu Hong, Julia Kreutzer, and Li Huang. 2020. KINNEWS and KIRNEWS:

Benchmarking cross-lingual text classification for Kinyarwanda and Kirundi. In *Proceedings of the 28th International Conference on Computational Linguistics*, pages 5507–5521, Barcelona, Spain (Online). International Committee on Computational Linguistics.

Iyanuoluwa Shode, David Ifeoluwa Adelani, and Anna Feldman. 2022. YOSM: A NEW YORUBA SENTIMENT CORPUS FOR MOVIE REVIEWS. In *3rd Workshop on African Natural Language Processing*.

Aditya Siddhant and Zachary C. Lipton. 2018. Deep bayesian active learning for natural language processing: Results of a large-scale empirical study.

Justin S. Smith, Benjamin Tyler Nebgen, Nick Lubbers, Olexandr Isayev, and Adrian E. Roitberg. 2018. Less is more: sampling chemical space with active learning. *The Journal of chemical physics*, 148 24:241733.

Manuel Tonneau, Dhaval Adjodah, Joao Palotti, Nir Grinberg, and Samuel Fraiberger. 2022. Multilingual detection of personal employment status on Twitter. In *Proceedings of the 60th Annual Meeting of the Association for Computational Linguistics (Volume 1: Long Papers)*, pages 6564–6587, Dublin, Ireland. Association for Computational Linguistics.

Ashish Vaswani, Noam Shazeer, Niki Parmar, Jakob Uszkoreit, Llion Jones, Aidan N Gomez, Ł ukasz Kaiser, and Illia Polosukhin. 2017. Attention is all you need. In *Advances in Neural Information Processing Systems*, volume 30. Curran Associates, Inc.

Guillaume Wenzek, Marie-Anne Lachaux, Alexis Conneau, Vishrav Chaudhary, Francisco Guzmán, Armand Joulin, and Edouard Grave. 2019. Ccnet: Extracting high quality monolingual datasets from web crawl data.

Thomas Wolf, Lysandre Debut, Victor Sanh, Julien Chaumond, Clement Delangue, Anthony Moi, Pierric Cistac, Tim Rault, Rémi Louf, Morgan Funtowicz, Joe Davison, Sam Shleifer, Patrick von Platen, Clara Ma, Yacine Jernite, Julien Plu, Canwen Xu, Teven Le Scao, Sylvain Gugger, Mariama Drame, Quentin Lhoest, and Alexander M. Rush. 2019. Huggingface's transformers: State-of-the-art natural language processing.

Linting Xue, Noah Constant, Adam Roberts, Mihir Kale, Rami Al-Rfou, Aditya Siddhant, Aditya Barua, and Colin Raffel. 2021. mt5: A massively multilingual pre-trained text-to-text transformer. In *NAACL*.

Yukun Zhu, Ryan Kiros, Rich Zemel, Ruslan Salakhutdinov, Raquel Urtasun, Antonio Torralba, and Sanja Fidler. 2015. Aligning books and movies: Towards story-like visual explanations by watching movies and reading books. In *The IEEE International Conference on Computer Vision (ICCV)*.

A Language Characteristics

Amharic (amh) also called Amarinya or Amerigna, is a Semitic language, an official language of Ethiopia, and is also spoken in Eritrea. Amharic is written with a modified version of the Ge'ez script, known as Fidel, consisting of 33 basic characters, each of them with at least 7 vowel sequences. Unlike Central and Northwest Semitic languages such as Arabic, Hebrew and Assyrian Aramaic, Amharic is written from left to right. The language has a variety of local dialects, all of which are mutually intelligible. There are three major dialects: Gondar, Gojjami, and Showa. There are specially marked differences in pronunciation, vocabulary, and grammar between the northern Gojjami and the southern Showa dialects.

Afan Oromo (oro) is an Afroasiatic language that belongs to the Cushitic branch spoken by about 30 million people in Ethiopia, Kenya, Somalia and Egypt, and it is the third largest language in Africa. The Oromo people are the largest ethnic group in Ethiopia and account for more than 40% of the population. They can be found all over Ethiopia, and particularly in Wollega, Shoa, Illubabour, Jimma, Arsi, Bale, Hararghe, Wollo, Borana and the southwestern part of Gojjam[2]. Afan Oromo is written with a Latin alphabet called Qubee. Like most other Ethiopian languages, whether Semitic, Cushitic, or Omotic, Oromo has a set of ejective consonants, that is, voiceless stops or affricates that are accompanied by glottalization and an explosive burst of air. Afan Oromo has another glottalized phone that is more unusual, an implosive retroflex stop, "dh" in Oromo orthography, a sound that is like an English "d" produced with the tongue curled back slightly and with the air drawn in so that a glottal stop is heard before the following vowel begins. It is retroflex in most dialects, though it is not strongly implosive and may reduce to a flap between vowels[3]. In the Qubee alphabet, letters include the digraphs ch, dh, ny, ph, sh. Gemination is not obligatorily marked for digraphs, though some writers indicate it by doubling the first element: qopphaa'uu 'be prepared'. Afan Oromo has five vowel phonemes, i.e., sounds that can differentiate word meaning. They can be short or long. The length of the vowel makes a difference in word meaning e.g., laga 'river' and laagaa 'roof of the

[2]https://omniglot.com/writing/oromo.htm

[3]`https://en.wikipedia.org/wiki/Oromo_language`

mouth'. Afan Oromo has 25 consonant phonemes, i.e., sounds that make a difference in word meaning. Like its close relative, Somali, native Oromo words do not have the consonants /p/, /v/, and /z/.

Bambara (bam) is a Western Mande language with about 14 million speakers mainly in Mali, and also in Senegal, Niger, Mauritania, Gambia and Côte d'Ivoire. It is spoken principally among the Bambara ethnic group in Mali, where it is the national language and the most widely understood one. Bambara is usually written with the Latin alphabet, though the N'Ko and Arabic alphabets are also used to some extent. It uses seven vowels a, e, ɛ, i, o, ɔ, and u each of which can be nasalized, pharyngealized and murmured, giving a total number of 21 vowels.

Ghomalá' (bbj) is a major Bamileke language of spoken in Cameroon. It is spoken by an estimated 1.1 million people in two main population groups.

Éwé (ewe) is a language spoken in Togo and southeastern Ghana by approximately 20 million people mainly in West Africa in the countries of Ghana, Togo, and Benin. It is recognised as a national language in Ghana, where English is the official language, and in Togo, where French is the official language. 'Ewe' is also the name of the tribal group that speaks this language. Éwé has three distinguishable dialects. Most of the differences among the dialects have to do with phonology. All dialects are mutually intelligible. Éwé is written in the African reference alphabet, first proposed by a UNESCO-organized conference in 1978. It is a version of the Latin alphabet adapted to represent Éwé sounds. Some sounds are represented by two-letter sequences, e.g., dz, ts, gb, kp, ny. Éwé has seven oral and five nasal vowels. Nasal vowels are produced by lowering the soft palate so that air escapes both through the mouth and the nose. Nasal vowels are marked by a tilde.

Fon (fon) also known as Fongbé is a native language of Benin Republic. It is spoken in average by 1.7 million people. Fon belongs to the *Niger-Congo-Gbe* languages family. It is a tonal, isolating and left-behind language according to (Joshi et al., 2020), with an *Subject-Verb-Object* (SVO) word order. Fon has about 53 different dialects, spoken throughout Benin (Lefebvre and Brousseau, 2002; Capo, 1991; Eberhard et al., 2020). Its alphabet is based on the Latin alphabet, with the addition of the letters: ɔ, ɗ, ɛ, and the digraphs gb, hw, kp, ny, and xw. There are 10 vowels phonemes in Fon: 6 said to be closed [i, u, ĩ, ũ], and 4 said to be opened [ɛ, ɔ, a, ã]. There are 22 consonants (m, b, n, ɗ, p, t, d, c, j, k, g, kp, gb, f, v, s, z, x, h, xw, hw, w). Fon has two phonemic tones: high and low. High is realized as rising *(low–high)* after a consonant. Basic disyllabic words have all four possibilities: *high-high*, *high-low*, *low-high*, and *low-low*. In longer phonological words, like verb and noun phrases, a high tone tends to persist until the final syllable. If that syllable has a phonemic low tone, it becomes falling *(high–low)*. Low tones disappear between high tones, but their effect remains as a downstep. Rising tones *(low–high)* simplify to high after high (without triggering downstep) and to low before high (Lefebvre and Brousseau, 2002; Capo, 1991).

Hausa (hau) belongs to the West Chadic branch of the Afro-Asiatic language family. It is one of the largest languages on the African continent, spoken as a first language by the original Hausa people and by people of Fula ancestry. Hausa is the majority language of much of northern Nigeria and the neighboring Republic of Niger. In addition, there is a sizable Hausa-speaking community in Sudan[4]. It has an alphabet of 29 letters containing 5 vowels and 24 consonants. Hausa alphabet is a Latin script/Roman alphabet/English letters except (x, v, p, and q) and also added six extra letters (ɓ, ɗ, ƙ, sh, ts and ƴ) (Adelani et al., 2021b). Hausa is an agglutinative language, i.e., it adds suffixes to roots for expressing grammatical relations without fusing them into one unit, as is the case in Indo-European languages.

Ìgbò (ibo) is one of the largest languages of West Africa, is spoken by 18 million people in Nigeria. It belongs to the Benue-Congo group of the Niger-Congo language family. The language is thought to have originated around the 9th century AD in the area near the confluence of the Niger and Benue rivers, and then spread over a wide area of southeastern Nigeria [5]. Igbo is a national language of Nigeria and is also recognised in Equatorial Guinea. Igbo is written in an expanded version of the Latin alphabet. Igbo is made up of many different dialects which aren't mutually intelligible to other Igbo speakers at times.

[4]https://www.mustgo.com/worldlanguages/hausa/
[5]https://www.mustgo.com/worldlanguages/igbo/

Kinyarwanda (kin) a is part of the Bantu subgroup of the central branch of the Niger-Congo language family. It is closely related to Kirundi, the language of Burundi. The Rwanda language is mutually intelligible with Kirundi, which is spoken in neighboring Burundi[6]. It has only 18/19 consonants, as X and Q are not found in the alphabet. L is often replaced by R, but due to the appearance of imported words in the language, that is not always the case. It has five vowel phonemes, i.e., sounds that make a difference in word meaning.

Lingala (lin) is a Central Bantu language that belongs to the largest African languages phylum: the Niger-Congo. Lingala is spoken as a first, second, and third language primarily in the Democratic Republic of Congo (DRC), the Republic of Congo (Congo-Brazzaville), and in parts of five neighboring central African states: Northwestern Angola, eastern Gabon, southern Central African Republic, and southwestern Sudan. The estimated number of speakers ranges from twenty to twenty five million[7]. It is written with the Latin alphabet. The seven vowels are represented by five symbols. The orthographic symbols 'e' and 'o' each represent two sounds. There are two tones in Lingala. High tone is represented with an acute accent, while low tone is unmarked.

Luganda (lug) is a Bantu language spoken in the African Great Lakes region. It is one of the major languages in Uganda and is spoken by more than 10 million Baganda and other people principally in central Uganda including the capital Kampala of Uganda. Its alphabet is composed of twenty-four letters; 18 consonants (b, p, v, f, m, d, t, l, r, n, z, s, j, c, g, k, ny, ŋ), 5 vowels (a, e, i, o, u) and 2 semi-vowels(w, y). Since the last consonant ŋ) does not appear on standard typewriters or computer keyboards, it is often replaced by the combination ng'. All consonants are pronounced as if with letter 'a' or 'ah' at the end. For example, bah, cah, jah, gah, kah, mah, pah, lah, zah, e.t.c

Luo (luo) are spoken by the Luo peoples in an area ranging from southern Sudan to southern Kenya, with Dholuo extending into northern Tanzania and Alur into the Democratic Republic of the Congo. Luo has a CVC or VC structure—consonant/vowel/consonant or vowel/consonant. This means that Luo words can end in a consonant, like gin, they are. This is unlike Bantu languages, where words must end in a vowel. Luo language is, therefore, more similar to English articulation, while Bantu languages are more like Italian[8].

Mooré (mos) is a Gur language of the Oti–Volta branch and one of two official regional languages of Burkina Faso. It is the language of the Mossi people, spoken by approximately 8 million people in Burkina Faso, plus another 1M+ in surrounding countries such as Ghana, Cote D'ivoire, Niger, Mali and Togo as a native language, but with many more L2 speakers. Mooré is spoken as a first or second language by over 50% of the Burkinabè population.

Chewa (nya) is a Bantu language spoken in much of Southern, Southeast and East Africa, namely the countries of Malawi and Zambia, where it is an official language, and Mozambique and Zimbabwe where it is a recognised minority language. Chewa has five vowel sounds: /a, ɛ, i, ɔ, u/; these are written a, e, i, o, u.

Naija (pcm) is an English-based creole language spoken as a lingua franca across Nigeria. The language is sometimes referred to as "Pijin" or Broken (pronounced "Brokun").

Shona (sna) is a Bantu language of the Shona people of Zimbabwe. All syllables in Shona end in a vowel. Consonants belong to the next syllable. For example, mangwanani ("morning") is syllabified as ma.ngwa.na.ni; "Zimbabwe" is zi.mba.bwe. No silent letters are used in Shona.

Swahili (swa) also known by its native name Kiswahili, is a Bantu language and the native language of the Swahili people native primarily to Tanzania. Swahili has become a second language spoken by tens of millions in four African Great Lakes countries (Kenya, DRC, Uganda, and Tanzania), where it is an official or national language, while being the first language for many people in Tanzania especially in the coastal regions of Tanga, Pwani, Dar es Salaam, Mtwara and Lindi. Standard Swahili has five vowel phonemes: /a/, /ɛ/, /i/, /ɔ/, and /u/.

Setswana (tsn) is a Bantu language spoken in Southern Africa by about 14 million people.

[6]https://nalrc.indiana.edu/doc/brochures/kinyarwanda.pdf

[7]https://nalrc.indiana.edu/doc/brochures/lingala.pdf

[8]https://owlcation.com/humanities/Luo-language-of-Kenya-Conversation-Basics

Setswana is an official language and lingua franca of Botswana and South Africa.

Akan/Twi is a dialect of the Akan language spoken in southern and central Ghana by several million people, mainly of the Akan people, the largest of the seventeen major ethnic groups in Ghana. Twi excludes consonants such as c, j, q, v, x and z. It has 15 consonants and 7 vowels. Apart from [a], [e], [i], [o] and [u], Twi also has 2 additional vowels; [ɛ] and [ɔ].

Wolof (wol) is a language of Senegal, Mauritania, and the Gambia, and the native language of the Wolof people. Wolof is the most widely spoken language in Senegal, spoken natively by the Wolof people (40% of the population) but also by most other Senegalese as a second language.

Xhosa (xho) also isiXhosa as an endonym, is a Nguni language and one of the official languages of South Africa and Zimbabwe. The Xhosa language employs 26 letters from the Latin alphabet. Xhosa has an inventory of ten vowels: [a], [ɛ e], [i], [ɔ o] and [u] written a, e, i, o and u in order, all occurring in both long and short. The /i/ vowel will be long in the penultimate syllable and short in the last syllable.

Yorùbá (yor) has 25 Latin letters without the Latin characters (c, q, v, x and z) and with additional letters (ẹ, gb,ṣ, ọ).Yorùbá is a tonal language with three tones: low ("\"), middle ("—", optional) and high ("/"). The Latin letters ⟨c⟩, ⟨q⟩, ⟨v⟩, ⟨x⟩, ⟨z⟩ are not used as part of the official orthography of Standard Yorùbá, however, they exist in several Yorùbá dialects. The tonal marks and underdots are referred to as diacritics and they are needed for the correct pronunciation of a word. Yorùbá is a highly isolating language and the sentence structure follows subject-verb-object (Adelani et al., 2021b).

Zulu (zul) is the mother tongue of the Zulu people, South's Africa largest ethnic group, who created an empire in the 19th century.Zulu has a 7-vowel system. Each vowel can be long or short. Zulu has close to 50 consonants including clicks, ejectives and implosives. Clicks originated in Khoisan languages and then spread into some neighboring Bantu ones. In Zulu they have three places of articulation: central alveolar, lateral alveolar and palatal combined with five accompaniments (plain, aspirated, voiced, nasal, and voiced nasal).

Towards Fair Supervised Dataset Distillation for Text Classification

Xudong Han[1] **Aili Shen**[1,2*] **Yitong Li**[3] **Lea Frermann**[1]
Timothy Baldwin[1,4] **Trevor Cohn**[1]
[1]The University of Melbourne [2]Alexa AI, Amazon
[3]Huawei Technologies Co., Ltd. [4]MBZUAI
xudonghl@student.unimelb.edu.au aili.shen@amazon.com
liyitong3@huawei.com {lfrermann,tbaldwin,t.cohn}@unimelb.edu.au

Abstract

With the growing prevalence of large-scale language models, their energy footprint and potential to learn and amplify historical biases are two pressing challenges. Dataset distillation (DD) — a method for reducing the dataset size by learning a small number of synthetic samples which encode the information in the original dataset — is a method for reducing the cost of model training, however its impact on fairness has not been studied. We investigate how DD impacts on group bias in the context of text classification tasks, with experiments over two data sets, concluding that vanilla DD preserves the bias of the dataset. We then show how existing debiasing methods can be combined with DD to produce models that are fair and accurate, at reduced training cost.[1]

1 Introduction

Training and inference with deep neural networks is generally costly in terms of storage and computing resources. Model compression methods such as knowledge distillation (Hinton et al., 2015) and pruning (Cheong and Daniel, 2019) are popular ways of reducing model size to make inference more efficient. An alternative approach is dataset distillation ("DD": Wang et al. (2018)), which compresses the training set into a small synthetic dataset. Although there is significant pre-cost associated with DD in learning synthetic instances, DD has been shown to achieve almost identical performance to training over the original training set (Wang et al., 2018), at reduced computational cost. For example, Sucholutsky and Schonlau show that, on the IMDB binary sentiment classification dataset (Maas et al., 2011), a randomly initialized model trained over the distilled dataset with 10 instances per class achieves almost 97.8% of the original accuracy.

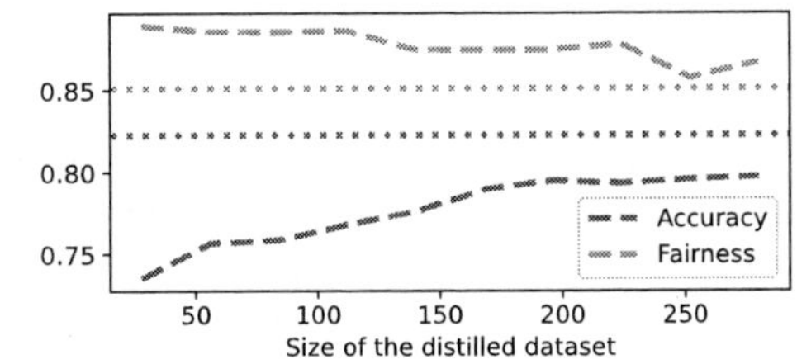

Figure 1: Performance and fairness over an occupation classification task, using models trained over the original (dotted lines) and distilled datasets (dashed lines) with different data sizes. For both metrics, larger is better. See Section 3.2 for full results.

It is well known that naively-trained models learn and amplify dataset biases, potentially leading to discrimination such as opportunity inequality (De-Arteaga et al., 2019). With the potential for compression methods to reduce training and storage cost, it is important to study their impact on model *fairness*. Here, we take DD as a case study and ask: (a) how does DD impact fairness; and (b) can we ensure fairness within this paradigm?

Specifically, we investigate how DD impacts on group fairness, and present experiments over two fairness benchmark datasets for text classification. Our contributions are: (1) we show that while DD preserves model performance, it also retains the dataset bias (e.g., Figure 1); and (2) we combine bias mitigation approaches with DD, and show that they improve fairness substantially.

2 Methodology

2.1 Dataset Distillation

Under STANDARD training, given inputs $\mathbf{x}$ annotated with main task labels $\mathbf{y}$ and protected labels $\mathbf{g}$, a neural network with parameters θ and loss function $\ell(\mathbf{x}, \mathbf{y}, \theta)$ learns $\theta^*=\arg\min_\theta \ell(\mathbf{x}, \mathbf{y}, \theta)$. Training with stochastic gradient descent (SGD) involves repeatedly sampling mini-batches of train-

*This work was done when Aili Shen was at The University of Melbourne.

[1]Source code available at `https://github.com/HanXudong/Fair_Dataset_Distillation`

Proceedings of The Third Workshop on Simple and Efficient Natural Language Processing (SustaiNLP), pages 65 - 72
December 7, 2022 ©2022 Association for Computational Linguistics

ing data and updating network parameters based on their error gradient scaled by learning rate η, i.e., $\theta_{t+1} = \theta_t - \eta \nabla_{\theta_t} \ell(\mathbf{x}_t, \mathbf{y}_t, \theta_t)$.

With DD (Wang et al., 2018) the goal is to find a synthetic dataset such that SGD results in a parameter update that maximally improves the STANDARD training loss. This works by starting with initial parameters θ_0 and optimising:

$$\tilde{\mathbf{x}}^*, \tilde{\mathbf{y}}^*, \tilde{\eta}^* = \arg\min_{\tilde{\mathbf{x}}, \tilde{\mathbf{y}}, \tilde{\eta}} \ell\left(\mathbf{x}, \mathbf{y}, \theta_0 - \tilde{\eta} \nabla_{\theta_0} \ell(\tilde{\mathbf{x}}, \tilde{\mathbf{y}}, \theta_0)\right) \quad (1)$$

where the inner gradient term is the SGD update on synthetic data, and the outer-most loss is the STANDARD loss using the resulting parameter update. The synthetic data instances, $\tilde{\mathbf{x}}$, their labels, $\tilde{\mathbf{y}}$ (represented softly, using a softmax parameterisation; Sucholutsky and Schonlau (2021)), and the learning rate, $\tilde{\eta}$, are learned using gradient descent over Equation (1). This requires twice differentiable ℓ; see Wang et al. (2018) and Sucholutsky and Schonlau (2021) for full details of the training algorithm. The final step after learning this small synthetic dataset (typically in the realm of 10-100 examples) is to use it to train a new model, which we can then evaluate for accuracy (as in prior work), and fairness (unique to this work).

Note that the distillation computational cost scales positively with both the synthetic dataset size, and the size of the original training set. In Section 3.2, we provide the average runtime for DD. When retraining networks over the distilled instances, the original dataset will not be used and is irrelevant to the retraining cost.

2.2 Bias Mitigation

Previously proposed bias mitigation approaches can be classified as: (a) *pre-processing* the dataset before training (Wang et al., 2019; Han et al., 2021a); (b) adjusting the training algorithm itself *at-training* (Li et al., 2018; Shen et al., 2021); and (c) *post-processing* the trained models (Bolukbasi et al., 2016; Ravfogel et al., 2020), which is less relevant here, as it obscures the effect of DD itself. To learn fairer distilled datasets, we employ a pre-processing method and an at-training method *at distillation time*; no further debiasing is applied at model training. We compare performance and bias of a naively-trained model on distilled data (a) without debiasing and (b) with debiased distillation using one of the methods described next.

Balanced Training for Equal Opportunity Fairness (BTEO) Recall that DD learns the compressed synthetic training set from the original dataset. Intuitively, we would expect to learn a fairer synthetic dataset if the original dataset is balanced w.r.t. the classes and protected attribute(s), which we can achieve by pre-processing the dataset ($\mathbf{x}$, $\mathbf{y}$ and $\mathbf{g}$). BTEO implements equal opportunity fairness by balancing the distribution of protected attributes for each class (Han et al., 2021a).

We achieve the objective of BTEO by dataset downsampling, which essentially creates a balanced training set where each demographic group has the same number of training instances per class.

Adversarial Training (ADV) Following the setup of Elazar and Goldberg (2018); Li et al. (2018); Han et al. (2021c), the optimisation objective for standard adversarial training is:

$$\min_{\theta} \max_{\phi} \ell(\mathbf{y}, \hat{\mathbf{y}}) - \lambda \ell(\mathbf{g}, \hat{\mathbf{g}}) \quad (2)$$

where ϕ denotes the trainable parameters of the adversary, and λ is a trade-off hyperparameter. Solving this minimax optimization problem encourages the main task model hidden representations to be informative w.r.t. $\mathbf{y}$ but uninformative w.r.t. $\mathbf{g}$.

In terms of the ADV for DD debiasing, the optimization for DD (Equation (1)) is combined with the adversarial loss (Equation (2)), resulting in the minimax problem,

$$\min_{\tilde{\mathbf{x}}, \tilde{\mathbf{y}}, \tilde{\eta}} \max_{\phi} [\ell\left(\mathbf{x}, \mathbf{y}, \theta_0 - \tilde{\eta} \nabla_{\theta_0} \ell(\tilde{\mathbf{x}}, \tilde{\mathbf{y}}, \theta_0)\right) - \lambda \ell(\mathbf{g}, \hat{\mathbf{g}})] \quad (3)$$

Similar to STANDARD +ADV, DD +ADV trains ϕ to predict $\hat{\mathbf{g}}$ over the final hidden representations of the real dataset ($\mathbf{x}$ and $\mathbf{g}$) extracted from the classifer. However, for DD, the classifier is trained over the synthetic datasets ($\tilde{\mathbf{x}}$ and $\tilde{\mathbf{y}}$). To decouple the training of model and discriminator, instead of solving the minimax problem with a gradient reversal layer (Ganin et al., 2016), we employ a two-step update following Han et al. (2021b). The negative sign for the adversarial loss ensures that adversary gradients are incorporated into DD to remove information related to protected attributes from the synthetic instances. For full details, see lines 6–9 of Algorithm 1 in Appendix A.

3 Experiments

In this section, we report experimental results for DD without and with debiasing. In Appendix B,

Model	MOJI			BIOS		
	Accuracy↑	Fairness↑	DTO↓	Accuracy↑	Fairness↑	DTO↓
STANDARD	72.3 ±0.5	61.2 ± 1.4	47.7	82.3 ±0.2	85.1 ±0.8	23.2
STANDARD + BTEO	75.4 ±0.1	87.7 ± 0.4	27.5	**83.8** ±0.2	90.5 ±0.9	**18.7**
STANDARD + ADV	75.6 ±0.7	**89.3** ± 0.6	**26.6**	81.7 ±0.2	**90.7** ±0.8	20.5
DD	71.3 ±1.8	62.4 ± 5.9	47.3	79.7 ±0.4	86.7 ±1.4	24.3
DD + BTEO	**75.7** ±0.4	88.8 ± 1.1	26.8	73.2 ±3.2	**90.7** ±1.3	28.3
DD + ADV	72.8 ±1.5	70.7 ± 9.1	40.0	80.3 ±0.5	87.7 ±1.2	23.2

Table 1: Evaluation results ± standard deviation (%) on the test set of sentiment analysis (MOJI) and biography classification (BIOS) tasks, averaged over 5 runs with different random seeds.

we provide full experimental details.

3.1 Experiment Setup

Dataset: We consider two tasks: (1) binary sentiment analysis over the MOJI dataset (Blodgett et al., 2016), with protected "race" attributes (African American English vs. Standard American English); and (2) 28-way occupation classification with protected attribute gender (Male vs. Female) for each biography (De-Arteaga et al., 2019).

Text DD: In order to perform text DD, we follow Sucholutsky and Schonlau (2021) in learning synthetic samples from the embedding space. Specifically, we create the training set by extracting document embeddings from a fixed pretrained language model, such that the learned synthetic 'documents' are vectors rather than text inputs.

Models: Since the inputs to DD are document representations from a pretrained model, we follow the typical classification head setting (Felbo et al., 2017; Devlin et al., 2019) in using a multi-layer perceptron classifer as the model (θ) for DD that is trained over distilled instances $\tilde{\mathbf{x}}$ and $\tilde{\mathbf{y}}$. Note that the parameter initialization is assumed to be known in this paper, which is the basic setting in Sucholutsky and Schonlau (2021). Specifically, θ_0 values are randomly sampled from Xavier Normal distribution (Glorot and Bengio, 2010), and are then repeatedly used in learning synthetic datasets and retraining the model over distilled datasets.

Evaluation Metrics: Following Ravfogel et al. (2020), we use overall accuracy as the performance metric, and the equal opportunity criterion (Hardt et al., 2016) to measure fairness in the form of the absolute recall differences (RD) between demographic groups. For ease of exposition, we report fairness as $1-\text{RD}$, where larger is better and a perfectly fair model will achieve a score of 1.

In addition to reporting performance and fairness metrics separately, we also report distance to the optimal point ("DTO"), which quantifies the accuracy–fairness tradeoff (Marler and Arora, 2004; Han et al., 2021a). DTO measures the normalized Euclidean distance for a given combination of accuracy and fairness to the optimal point which denotes the ideal result, e.g., accuracy and fairness of 1.0. It is typically unachievable in practice.

Training Details: We follow Sucholutsky and Schonlau (2021) in our hyperparameter settings for text DD. Specifically, we conduct distillation for 10 GD steps, with 3 epochs for each iteration. Within each step, we generate one synthetic text embedding per target class, resulting in a total of 20 (= 10 steps $\times$ 2 classes) and 280 (= 10 steps $\times$ 28 classes) synthetic embeddings for MOJI and BIOS, respectively.

3.2 Results and Analysis

Table 1 summarizes the experimental results. STANDARD model is trained over the original training set without debiasing, while DD denotes models with the same architecture as STANDARD but trained over the distilled synthetic dataset. Over both datasets, DD achieves similar accuracy to STANDARD, consistent with previous work (Wang et al., 2018; Sucholutsky and Schonlau, 2021).

How does DD impact fairness? Similar patterns are observed over both datasets that fairness improves marginally: models trained over the distilled datasets retained 97.9% and 89.2% of the bias for MOJI and BIOS, respectively.

Can we ensure fairness of DD? As described in Section 2.2, we combined DD with two debiasing methods: BTEO (Han et al., 2021a) and ADV (Li et al., 2018). The methods are used only at the distillation stage, and not when training models over

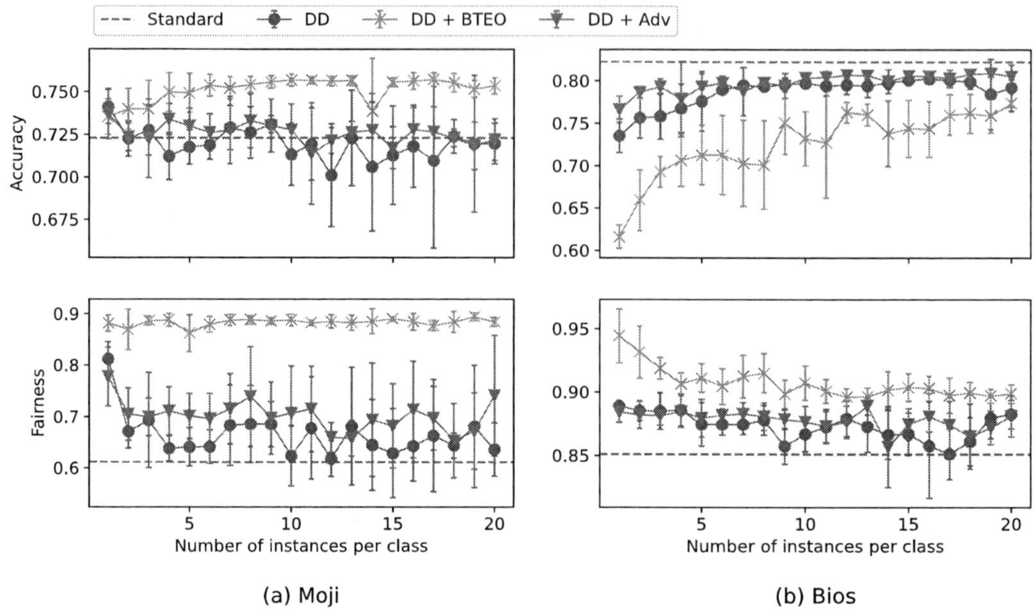

Figure 2: Evaluation results ± standard deviation with respect to different distilled dataset sizes.

the distilled dataset. Table 1 shows that, over the MOJI dataset, both STANDARD +BTEO and STANDARD +ADV improve fairness while also achieving better accuracy, leading to better performance–fairness trade-off (smaller DTO). This is consistent with previous work (Han et al., 2021c). Both debiasing methods substantially improve fairness while retaining accuracy compared to DD, with DD +BTEO being most effective.

In terms of BIOS, the fairness of DD +BTEO improves while accuracy drops appreciably, combining to result in a worse DTO. Since BIOS is a multiclass dataset with label skew, this is largely due to the naive sampling strategy of BTEO. Specifically, as suggested by Sucholutsky and Schonlau (2021), DD is less efficient for complex tasks, and we hypothesise the number of distilled instances for BIOS is insufficient for BTEO which additionally prevents the classifier from leaning unwanted correlations by manipulating the training dataset. DD +ADV, on the other hand, also improves fairness while retaining similar accuracy to DD.

Varying the size of distilled dataset To better understand the influence of the number of instances per class (= steps) in DD without explicit debiasing, we vary the number of steps from 1 to 20 (Figure 2). As the number of instances per class decreases, the accuracy drops substantially over BIOS, but stays relatively constant over MOJI, again implying that BIOS is a more challenging dataset than MOJI, due to the combination of the much larger label set and skew. Fairness scores generally increase as the number of instances per class decreases, but the combined DTO results are below the debiasing approaches at the same fairness level.

As for DD +BTEO over the BIOS set, the accuracy increases monotonically as the distilled dataset size increases, confirming our previous hypothesis that 10 instances per class is insufficient for BTEO.

Ultimately, the best choice of distilled dataset size is influenced by both the original task and the debiasing methods, and an important hyperparameter for DD debiasing that needs to be tuned jointly. For MOJI, an overly-large number of instances per class leads to worse performance and instability, while the harder task BIOS is more stable than MOJI given the same conditions, consisting with the previous work (Wang et al., 2018).

Training cost of DD Similar to pre-training, DD incurs a one-time cost in generating the distilled dataset. However, the computational cost of DD can be much more expensive than training the same model over the original datasets. Tables 2a and 2b show the computational cost for DD in seconds over MOJI and BIOS, respectively.

Table 3 compares the training time for the non-DD methods with DD (with 10 instances per class) over the two datasets. ADV incurs additional cost

Size	Distillation			Train
	DD	DD + ADV	DD + BTEO	
1	144	139	74	< 0.5
2	195	203	95	< 0.5
3	252	259	115	< 0.5
4	307	302	141	< 0.5
5	377	352	165	< 0.5
6	442	411	181	1
7	477	463	212	1
8	531	524	227	1
9	581	621	248	1
10	632	629	268	1
11	716	722	292	1
12	770	774	314	1
13	840	864	345	1
14	882	852	363	1
15	931	923	408	2
16	961	1051	417	2
17	998	991	438	2
18	1064	1052	473	2
19	1124	1158	488	2
20	1162	1268	525	2

(a) MOJI

Size	Distillation			Train
	DD	DD + ADV	DD + BTEO	
1	474	462	108	< 0.5
2	783	756	153	1
3	1137	1107	199	1
4	1459	1578	249	1
5	1919	1856	292	1
6	2325	2208	346	1
7	2485	2462	394	1
8	2802	2876	447	2
9	3037	3114	502	2
10	3453	3848	508	2
11	3769	3862	577	3
12	4225	4179	647	3
13	4620	4607	694	4
14	5370	4799	741	4
15	5084	5097	865	4
16	5442	6012	824	4
17	6139	6399	865	5
18	6007	6171	938	5
19	6685	6566	937	5
20	6728	6971	1025	5

(b) BIOS

Table 2: Computational cost (sec) to: (a) learn synthetic instances through distillation; and (b) train the model over the synthetic instances.

	Training Time	
Model	MOJI	BIOS
STANDARD	35	96
STANDARD + ADV	40	135
STANDARD + BTEO	19	32
DD	1	2

Table 3: Training time (sec) over MOJI and BIOS.

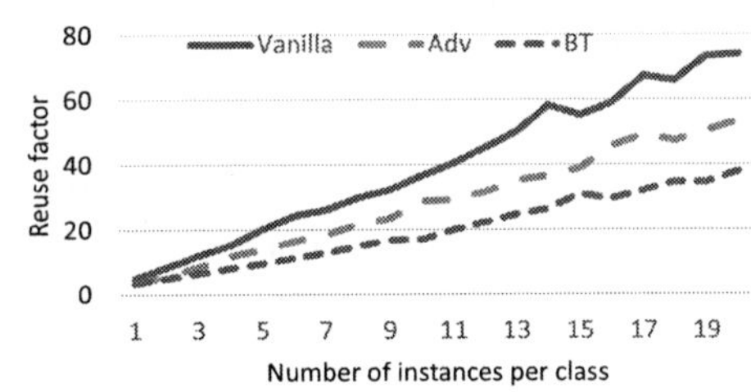

Figure 3: Reuse factor of DD on the BIOS dataset.

over STANDARD due to the discriminator training, while BTEO results in faster training due to the reduction in training set size.

In terms of DD, the debiasing is only employed as part of learning the synthetic instances, and does not affect the classifier training over the distilled dataset. As such, the training time for DD, DD + ADV, and DD + BTEO is identical. As it can be seen, training a model over a pre-distilled dataset is much faster than the STANDARD training, but when the combined cost of dataset distillation and model training is taken into account, it is around an order of magnitude slower than STANDARD training.

To further analysis how the upfront task of DD compares to the training cost, Figure 3 shows the reuse factor w.r.t. different DD sizes. For example, for a naively trained model, the reuse factor for size 10 is calculated as $\frac{3453}{96-2} \approx 36.73$, where 3453 and 2 are the distillation time and training time of DD w.r.t. size 10 (Table 2b), and 96 is the training time of STANDARD (Table 3). It can be seen that the ratio of neutralization and distilled dataset size are positively correlated, and debiasing methods (ADV and BTEO) requires less time to neutralize the pre-cost of DD.

4 Conclusion

This paper evaluated the effect of dataset distillation on fairness in the context of two text classification tasks. Empirically, we showed that distilled datasets retain unwanted biases. In order to learn fairer synthetic datasets, we employ adversarial learning and balanced training for bias mitigation, which results in substantial fairness improvements. We conclude that DD can be effective for fair *and* efficient text classification, specifically for simpler tasks where a small distilled data set is sufficient.

Acknowledgements

We thank the anonymous reviewers for their helpful feedback and suggestions. This work was funded by the Australian Research Council, Discovery grant DP200102519. This research was undertaken using the LIEF HPC-GPGPU Facility hosted at the University of Melbourne. This Facility was established with the assistance of LIEF Grant LE170100200.

Limitations

Hyperparameter Tuning Taking ADV debiasing as an example, the current practice is to finetune the trade-off hyperparameter to find the best-performing model. However, tuning the trade-off hyperparameter is too expensive for DD due to the high cost of distillation. In this paper, we assume that the trade-off hyperparameters for bias mitigation are only affected by the training dataset and model architecture. Based on this assumption, we adopted the best trade-off hyperparameter settings from STANDARD training for DD, but further exploration of this interaction is warranted in future work.

Parameter Initialization We adopted the DD framework of Sucholutsky and Schonlau (2021), including its strong assumptions about the initial parameters of the classifiers that are trained over the synthetic datasets. Specifically, the initial weights (θ_0) are assumed to be either fixed and known, or drawn from a fixed and known distribution, before and after distillation. This implies, for example, that the classifier architecture has to be the same as what was used during distillation. However, this assumption underlies most existing DD work, and is outside the scope of this research.

Ethical Considerations

This work aims to detect and mitigate bias in distilled datasets in NLP. For DD, both the distillation over original datasets and the classifier training over the distilled datasets do not access the protected attributes. However, consistent with previous work, the fairness definition and evaluation are based on the protected attributes. Briefly, the protected attributes are unobserved during distillation, model training, and inference, and are only used for evaluation purposes.

This work relies on benchmarks to evaluate model fairness and accuracy. Like much previous work, these benchmarks propose an oversimplified, binary notion of the protected attributes. We acknowledge that both gender (Sun et al., 2019) and race (Field et al., 2021) are more nuanced. As a result of such oversimplification specifically, and the controlled nature of benchmarks in general, we recommend to additionally consult user studies and application scenarios to obtain holistic measure of model fairness.

In terms of the DD debiasing, the employed method requires access to training datasets with protected attributes, consistent with previous work on adversarial training and other bias mitigation methods. After distillation, it is important to note that the model trained over the debiased distilled dataset can make fairer predictions without any requirement of demographic information for either synthetic instances or test instances.

We only use attributes that the user has self-identified in our experiments. All data in this study is publicly available and used under strict ethical guidelines.

References

Su Lin Blodgett, Lisa Green, and Brendan O'Connor. 2016. Demographic dialectal variation in social media: A case study of African-American English. In *Proceedings of the 2016 Conference on Empirical Methods in Natural Language Processing*, pages 1119–1130.

Tolga Bolukbasi, Kai-Wei Chang, James Y Zou, Venkatesh Saligrama, and Adam T Kalai. 2016. Man is to computer programmer as woman is to homemaker? debiasing word embeddings. In *Advances in Neural Information Processing Systems*, pages 4349–4357.

Robin Cheong and Robel Daniel. 2019. transformers.zip: Compressing transformers with pruning and quantization. *Technical report, Stanford University, Stanford, California*.

Maria De-Arteaga, Alexey Romanov, Hanna Wallach, Jennifer Chayes, Christian Borgs, Alexandra Chouldechova, Sahin Geyik, Krishnaram Kenthapadi, and Adam Tauman Kalai. 2019. Bias in bios: A case study of semantic representation bias in a high-stakes setting. In *Proceedings of the Conference on Fairness, Accountability, and Transparency*, pages 120–128.

Jacob Devlin, Ming-Wei Chang, Kenton Lee, and Kristina Toutanova. 2019. BERT: Pre-training of deep bidirectional transformers for language understanding. In *Proceedings of the 2019 Conference of the North American Chapter of the Association for*

Computational Linguistics: Human Language Technologies, Volume 1 (Long and Short Papers), pages 4171–4186.

Yanai Elazar and Yoav Goldberg. 2018. Adversarial removal of demographic attributes from text data. In *Proceedings of the 2018 Conference on Empirical Methods in Natural Language Processing*, pages 11–21.

Bjarke Felbo, Alan Mislove, Anders Søgaard, Iyad Rahwan, and Sune Lehmann. 2017. Using millions of emoji occurrences to learn any-domain representations for detecting sentiment, emotion and sarcasm. In *Conference on Empirical Methods in Natural Language Processing (EMNLP)*.

Anjalie Field, Su Lin Blodgett, Zeerak Waseem, and Yulia Tsvetkov. 2021. A survey of race, racism, and anti-racism in NLP. In *Proceedings of the 59th Annual Meeting of the Association for Computational Linguistics and the 11th International Joint Conference on Natural Language Processing (Volume 1: Long Papers)*, pages 1905–1925, Online. Association for Computational Linguistics.

Yaroslav Ganin, Evgeniya Ustinova, Hana Ajakan, Pascal Germain, Hugo Larochelle, François Laviolette, Mario Marchand, and Victor Lempitsky. 2016. Domain-adversarial training of neural networks. *The Journal of Machine Learning Research*, 17(1):2096–2030.

Xavier Glorot and Yoshua Bengio. 2010. Understanding the difficulty of training deep feedforward neural networks. In *Proceedings of the thirteenth international conference on artificial intelligence and statistics*, pages 249–256. JMLR Workshop and Conference Proceedings.

Xudong Han, Timothy Baldwin, and Trevor Cohn. 2021a. Balancing out bias: Achieving fairness through training reweighting. *arXiv preprint arXiv:2109.08253*.

Xudong Han, Timothy Baldwin, and Trevor Cohn. 2021b. Decoupling adversarial training for fair NLP. In *Findings of the Association for Computational Linguistics: ACL-IJCNLP 2021*, pages 471–477.

Xudong Han, Timothy Baldwin, and Trevor Cohn. 2021c. Diverse adversaries for mitigating bias in training. In *Proceedings of the 16th Conference of the European Chapter of the Association for Computational Linguistics: Main Volume*, pages 2760–2765.

Xudong Han, Aili Shen, Yitong Li, Lea Frermann, Timothy Baldwin, and Trevor Cohn. 2022. fairlib: A unified framework for assessing and improving classification fairness. *arXiv preprint arXiv:2205.01876*.

Moritz Hardt, Eric Price, and Nati Srebro. 2016. Equality of opportunity in supervised learning. *Advances in Neural Information Processing Systems*, 29:3315–3323.

Geoffrey Hinton, Oriol Vinyals, and Jeff Dean. 2015. Distilling the knowledge in a neural network. *arXiv preprint arXiv:1503.02531*, 2(7).

Yitong Li, Timothy Baldwin, and Trevor Cohn. 2018. Towards robust and privacy-preserving text representations. In *Proceedings of the 56th Annual Meeting of the Association for Computational Linguistics (Volume 2: Short Papers)*, pages 25–30.

Andrew Maas, Raymond E Daly, Peter T Pham, Dan Huang, Andrew Y Ng, and Christopher Potts. 2011. Learning word vectors for sentiment analysis. In *Proceedings of the 49th annual meeting of the association for computational linguistics: Human language technologies*, pages 142–150.

R Timothy Marler and Jasbir S Arora. 2004. Survey of multi-objective optimization methods for engineering. *Structural and Multidisciplinary Optimization*, 26(6):369–395.

Shauli Ravfogel, Yanai Elazar, Hila Gonen, Michael Twiton, and Yoav Goldberg. 2020. Null it out: Guarding protected attributes by iterative nullspace projection. In *Proceedings of the 58th Annual Meeting of the Association for Computational Linguistics*, pages 7237–7256.

Aili Shen, Xudong Han, Trevor Cohn, Timothy Baldwin, and Lea Frermann. 2021. Contrastive learning for fair representations. *arXiv preprint arXiv:2109.10645*.

Ilia Sucholutsky and Matthias Schonlau. 2021. Soft-label dataset distillation and text dataset distillation. In *2021 International Joint Conference on Neural Networks (IJCNN)*, pages 1–8. IEEE.

Tony Sun, Andrew Gaut, Shirlyn Tang, Yuxin Huang, Mai ElSherief, Jieyu Zhao, Diba Mirza, Elizabeth Belding, Kai-Wei Chang, and William Yang Wang. 2019. Mitigating gender bias in natural language processing: Literature review. In *Proceedings of the 57th Annual Meeting of the Association for Computational Linguistics*, pages 1630–1640, Florence, Italy. Association for Computational Linguistics.

Tianlu Wang, Jieyu Zhao, Mark Yatskar, Kai-Wei Chang, and Vicente Ordonez. 2019. Balanced datasets are not enough: Estimating and mitigating gender bias in deep image representations. In *Proceedings of the IEEE International Conference on Computer Vision*, pages 5310–5319.

Tongzhou Wang, Jun-Yan Zhu, Antonio Torralba, and Alexei A Efros. 2018. Dataset distillation. *arXiv preprint arXiv:1811.10959*.

Algorithm 1 Fair Dataset Distillation

Input: θ_0 = initial weights of the main model; α = DD step size; T = number of optimization iterations; $\tilde{y}_0$ = initial value for $\tilde{y}$; $\tilde{\eta}_0$ = initial value for $\tilde{\eta}$; λ = strength of the adversarial regularization

Initialize distilled dataset with M instances
  $\tilde{\mathbf{x}} = \{\tilde{x}_i\}_{i=1}^{M}$ randomly,
  $\tilde{\mathbf{y}} = \{\tilde{y}_i\}_{i=1}^{M} \leftarrow \tilde{y}_0$,
  $\tilde{\eta} \leftarrow \tilde{\eta}_0$
for each training step t = 1 to T **do**
  Get a mini-batch of n real training instances
    $(\mathbf{x}_t, \mathbf{y}_t) = \{x_{t,j}, y_{t,j}\}_{j=1}^{n}$
  Compute updated model parameters with GD
    $\theta_1 = \theta_0 - \tilde{\eta}\nabla_{\theta_0}\ell(\tilde{\mathbf{x}}, \tilde{\mathbf{y}}, \theta_0)$
  Evaluate the objective function on real training data:
    $\mathcal{L} = \ell(\mathbf{x}_t, \mathbf{y}_t, \theta_1)$
  if ADV **then**
    Update the discriminator ϕ
      $\phi = \phi - \eta_{\text{adv}}\nabla_{\phi}\ell(\mathbf{x}_t, \mathbf{g}_t, \theta_1, \phi)$
    Incorporate adversarial loss
      $\mathcal{L} = \mathcal{L} - \lambda\ell(\mathbf{x}_t, \mathbf{g}_t, \theta_1, \phi)$
  end if
  Update distilled data
    $\tilde{\mathbf{x}} \leftarrow \tilde{\mathbf{x}} - \alpha\nabla_{\tilde{\mathbf{x}}}\sum_j \mathcal{L}$,
    $\tilde{\mathbf{y}} \leftarrow \tilde{\mathbf{y}} - \alpha\nabla_{\tilde{\mathbf{y}}}\sum_j \mathcal{L}$,
    $\tilde{\eta} \leftarrow \tilde{\eta} - \alpha\nabla_{\tilde{\eta}}\sum_j \mathcal{L}$
end for

Output: distilled data $\tilde{\mathbf{x}}$; labels $\tilde{\mathbf{y}}$; and learning rate $\tilde{\eta}$

A Algorithm

The algorithm for combined DD with debiasing techniques is detailed in Algorithm 1.

B Experimental Details

B.1 Dataset Splits

We use the same data split as previous work (Ravfogel et al., 2020), resulting in train, dev, and test splits of 100k/8k/8k for MOJI, and 257k/40k/100k for BIOS.

B.2 Fairness Metric

We follow the previous work (Han et al., 2021c) in reporting the RMS recall (TPR) disparities. The calculation of RMS TPR GAP consists of aggregations at the group and class levels. At the group level, we measure the absolute TPR difference of each class between each group and the overall TPR $GAP_{G,y}^{TPR} = \sum_{g\in G} |TPR_{g,y} - TPR_y|$, and at the class level, we further perform the RMS aggregation at the class level to get the RMS TPR GAP as $GAP = \sqrt{\frac{1}{|Y|}\sum_{y\in Y}(GAP_{G,y}^{TPR})^2}$.

B.3 Models

We follow Ravfogel et al. (2020) in using DeepMoji (Felbo et al., 2017) as the encoder to get 2304d representations of the input texts. For the BIOS dataset, we follow Han et al. (2021a) in taking 768d 'AVG' representations from BERT-base (Devlin et al., 2019), which takes the average of all contextualized token embeddings.

The number of trainable parameters of the classifier is about 1M for both tasks. The synthetic datasets can also be treated as trained parameters, and the total number of trainable parameters are influenced by, dimension of the embedding space (nd), the number of classes (nc), and the number of distillation steps (ns), resulting in $ns \times (nd \times nc + nc \times nc + 1$, which are $4613 \times ns$ and $22289 \times ns$ for MOJI and BIOS, respectively.

We notice that DD is slow to converge for some random initializations. When running DD with different random seeds, we set dataset-specific accuracy thresholds to filter unconverged runs, which are 0.65 and 0.6 for MOJI and BIOS, respectively.

B.4 Computing Infrastructure

We conduct our experiments on a Windows server with a 16-core CPU (AMD Ryzen Threadripper PRO 3955WX), two NVIDIA GeForce RTX 3090s with NVLink, and 256GB RAM, and on a HPC cluster instance with 4 CPU cores, 32GB RAM, and one NVIDIA V100 GPU.

B.5 Hyperparameter Tuning

We use the same model architectures and hyperparameters as previous work (Han et al., 2022), which are shown to achieve better results than the results in the original paper of BTEO (Han et al., 2021a) and ADV (Li et al., 2018). We vary the size of the distilled dataset from 1 to 20 for each method and run experiments 7 times with different random seeds for each hyperparameter combination. Corresponding scripts are included in the submitted code file.

Author Index